T0338000

THE
CONCEPTUAL
FOUNDATIONS
OF
INVESTING

THE
CONCEPTUAL FOUNDATIONS
OF
INVESTING

A Short Book of Need-to-Know Essentials

Bradford Cornell
Shaun Cornell
Andrew Cornell

WILEY

Published by John Wiley & Sons, Inc., Hoboken, New Jersey.
Published simultaneously in Canada.

For general information on our other products and services or for technical support, please contact our
Customer Care Department within the United States at (800) 762–2974, outside the United States at
(317) 572–3993, or fax (317) 572–4002.

Wiley publishes in a variety of print and electronic formats and by print-on-demand. Some material
included with standard print versions of this book may not be included in e-books or in
print-on-demand. If this book refers to media such as a CD or DVD that is not included in the version
you purchased, you may download this material at http://booksupport.wiley.com. For more
information about Wiley products, visit www.wiley.com.

Library of Congress Cataloging-in-Publication Data

Names: Cornell, Bradford, author. | Cornell, Shaun, 1979– author. | Cornell,
   Andrew, 1981– author.
Title: The conceptual foundations of investing : a short book of need-to-know
   essentials / Bradford Cornell, Shaun Cornell, Andrew Cornell.
Description: First Edition. | Hoboken : Wiley, 2018. | Includes index. |
Identifiers: LCCN 2018021871 (print) | LCCN 2018025246 (ebook) |
   ISBN 9781119516323 (Adobe PDF) | ISBN 9781119516316 (ePub) |
   ISBN 9781119516293 (hardback)
Subjects: LCSH: Investments. | Finance, Personal. | BISAC: BUSINESS &
   ECONOMICS / Finance.
Classification: LCC HG4521 (ebook) | LCC HG4521 .C6597 2018 (print) |
   DDC 332.6—dc23
LC record available at https://lccn.loc.gov/2018021871

Cover Design: Wiley
Cover Image: © Lava 4 images/Shutterstock

Printed in the United States of America
V10003722_082218

CONTENTS

PREFACE

In the years following the development of the capital asset pricing model in 1964, research in finance has revolutionized the understanding of financial markets. The problem is that much of the research that produced that revolution is highly technical and mathematical, making it difficult for investors who are not experts to grasp the conceptual foundations on which the modern understanding of investing is based.

This book is designed to fill that gap. Its goal is to provide an understanding of the conceptual foundations of modern investment theory with a minimum of technical detail. For those interested in the more technical nuances, there are an excellent variety of textbooks used in business school classes worldwide from which to choose.

At the outset, it is important to recognize that the conceptual foundations to which we refer are not a series of tips for how to beat the market. In fact, one of the foundations, which we explain in detail, is that there can be no set of rules analogous to "Newton's laws" for beating the market. Ironically, Newton himself lost a fortune in the South Sea Bubble, leading him to state, "he could calculate the motions of the heavenly bodies, but not the madness of the people." What the foundations do is help you understand how investment markets function and how to avoid a wide variety of mistakes that less sophisticated investors commonly make.

The book is also designed to help investors ask the right questions about investing. In a sense, it can be thought of as a self-protection manual. Because there are tens of *trillions* of dollars invested worldwide, there are immense incentives to profit by gaining control over those funds, earning fees by managing those funds, and charging commissions for transactions involving those funds. The desire to reach and influence investors supports a huge financial media – some of it reputable and some of it not. In addition, there is massive amount of investment marketing. In our view, to cope with this information avalanche, investors must understand the conceptual foundations of investing with sufficient clarity to ensure that they will not be misled. This book is designed to provide that clarity.

A word of warning. While we avoid the complex mathematics that characterizes much of modern finance, understanding the conceptual foundations of investing does require getting your hands dirty working with investment data in spreadsheets. To help the reader in that regard, the spreadsheets that contain all the data in the exhibits presented in the book are available at www.wiley.com/go/CornellCFOI (Password: CFI). In addition, it is impossible to avoid a few equations and mathematical concepts. We hope that our explanations help those who are not mathematically inclined through those parts of the book.

Many investors may say that they do not need a personal understanding of the conceptual foundations of investing because they rely on investment advisors. Such reliance just pushes the questions back one step. How do you choose an investment advisor? How do you determine whether the advisor is giving you appropriate advice? How do you evaluate whether the advisory costs are reasonable? Answering such questions requires an understanding of the conceptual foundations of investing.

1

RETURNS

This is a book about the conceptual foundations of investing. That does not mean concepts for beating the market. In fact, one of the conceptual foundations that we will return to throughout the book is that there cannot be a trick for beating the market. If there were, and if the trick became well known, who would sell when the trick said buy? The best that can be hoped for is that a strategy for beating the market may work for a while as long as it is not widely known and adopted. Of course, no one would write a book about such a strategy; they would start an investment firm.

That does not mean that understanding the conceptual foundations of investing will not improve an investor's performance. There are a host of investment mistakes that can be avoided by such an understanding. One example involves the trade-off between risk and return. The trade-off seems to imply that if you bear more risk you will have higher long-run average returns. That conclusion is false. It is possible to bear a great deal of risk and get no benefit in terms of higher average return. Understanding the conceptual foundations of finance makes it clear why this is so and, thereby, helps an investor avoid bearing uncompensated risks.

Another choice every investor has to make is between active and passive investing. Making that choice wisely requires understanding the conceptual foundations of investing.

There are numerous other examples we could offer but we are getting ahead of ourselves. Before drawing conclusions, it is essential to lay the proper ground work. In finance and investing everything starts with the concept of returns. Just as the atom is the fundamental unit of analysis in chemistry, the return is the fundamental unit of analysis in investing. The first step in being able to analyze investing properly is becoming comfortable calculating and working with returns. For that reason, our book starts with returns.

The return on an investment is the percentage increase in your wealth associated with holding an investment for a given time period. For example, if you invest $10,000 and earn a 1% return your wealth has increased to $10,100. While this may seem entirely straightforward, much mischief can arise when calculating returns. Because they are the "atoms" of finance, it is critical to understand how returns are calculated and used before turning to more abstract concepts like expected returns or the trade-off between risk and expected return.

One convention we will follow throughout this book is that a "day" will always refer to a trading day. No distinction is drawn, for example, between the trading interval that runs from the close of Friday to the close on Monday as opposed to the close on Monday to the close on Tuesday. Both of these are treated as trading days. The same is true of holidays and three-day weekends. Using this convention, there are typically 252 trading days in a year.

Let's get started with an example. Be prepared to do a little math. There is more to returns than you might expect. The first column of Exhibit 1.1 presents the price of Apple stock for 42 trading days from January 3, 2017 to March 3, 2017. As the exhibit shows, this was a good two months for Apple. The price rose from $116.15 to $139.78.

The third column of the exhibit shows the percentage change in the price of Apple stock on a daily basis. A common mistake is to associate the percentage change in the price of a security with the return. The error is common because on most days it is not a mistake – the return and the percentage price change are the same. But not on every day. That is because Apple pays a dividend and that dividend is part of the return.

There is a problem incorporating the dividend when calculating the return. On what day do you add in the dividend? The obvious answer appears to be on the day it is paid, but that is wrong because markets are forward looking. The correct day is what is called the ex-dividend date (commonly referred to as the "ex-date"), which is the day after the day on which Apple checks its shareholder records to decide who gets the dividend. If you own Apple shares the day before the ex-date, you get the dividend. If you do not buy until the ex-date, you no longer get the dividend. Therefore, the price of the Apple shares drops by the amount of the dividend on the ex-date (holding other factors that may affect the price constant). This means the dividend should be added to the price change on the ex-dividend date when computing returns.

Dividends are not only source of income on securities; bonds typically make payments every six months and mortgages generally pay monthly. All these cash distributions must be taken account of to properly compute returns. This leads to the mathematical

EXHIBIT 1.1 Apple returns and path of wealth (POW).

(1)	(2)	(3)	(4)	(5)	(6)	(7)	(8)
Date	Apple closing price	Percentage price change (%)	Dividend and ex-date	Apple return (%)	Path of wealth – POW	Average return (%)	POW from average returns
1/3/2017	116.15				100.00		100.00
1/4/2017	116.02	−0.112		−0.112	99.89	0.469	100.47
1/5/2017	116.61	0.509		0.509	100.40	0.469	100.94
1/6/2017	117.91	1.115		1.115	101.52	0.469	101.41
1/9/2017	118.99	0.916		0.916	102.45	0.469	101.89
1/10/2017	119.11	0.101		0.101	102.55	0.469	102.37
1/11/2017	119.75	0.537		0.537	103.10	0.469	102.84
1/12/2017	119.25	−0.418		−0.418	102.67	0.469	103.33
1/13/2017	119.04	−0.176		−0.176	102.49	0.469	103.81
1/17/2017	120.00	0.806		0.806	103.31	0.469	104.30
1/18/2017	119.99	−0.008		−0.008	103.31	0.469	104.79
1/19/2017	119.78	−0.175		−0.175	103.13	0.469	105.28
1/20/2017	120.00	0.184		0.184	103.31	0.469	105.77
1/23/2017	120.08	0.067		0.067	103.38	0.469	106.27
1/24/2017	119.97	−0.092		−0.092	103.29	0.469	106.76
1/25/2017	121.88	1.592		1.592	104.93	0.469	107.26
1/26/2017	121.94	0.049		0.049	104.98	0.469	107.77
1/27/2017	121.95	0.008		0.008	104.99	0.469	108.27
1/30/2017	121.63	−0.262		−0.262	104.72	0.469	108.78
1/31/2017	121.35	−0.230		−0.230	104.48	0.469	109.29
2/1/2017	128.75	6.098		6.098	110.85	0.469	109.80
2/2/2017	128.53	−0.171		−0.171	110.66	0.469	110.32
2/3/2017	129.08	0.428		0.428	111.13	0.469	110.83
2/6/2017	130.29	0.937		0.937	112.17	0.469	111.35
2/7/2017	131.53	0.952		0.952	113.24	0.469	111.87
2/8/2017	132.04	0.388		0.388	113.68	0.469	112.40
2/9/2017	**132.42**	**0.288**	**0.57**	**0.719**	**114.50**	**0.469**	**112.93**
2/10/2017	132.12	−0.227		−0.227	114.24	0.469	113.45
2/13/2017	133.29	0.886		0.886	115.25	0.469	113.99
2/14/2017	135.02	1.298		1.298	116.75	0.469	114.52
2/15/2017	135.51	0.363		0.363	117.17	0.469	115.06
2/16/2017	135.35	−0.118		−0.118	117.03	0.469	115.60
2/17/2017	135.72	0.273		0.273	117.35	0.469	116.14
2/21/2017	136.70	0.722		0.722	118.20	0.469	116.68
2/22/2017	137.11	0.300		0.300	118.55	0.469	117.23
2/23/2017	136.53	−0.423		−0.423	118.05	0.469	117.78
2/24/2017	136.66	0.095		0.095	118.16	0.469	118.33
2/27/2017	136.93	0.198		0.198	118.40	0.469	118.88
2/28/2017	136.99	0.044		0.044	118.45	0.469	119.44

EXHIBIT 1.1 (Continued)

(1)	(2)	(3)	(4)	(5)	(6)	(7)	(8)
Date	Apple closing price	Percentage price change (%)	Dividend and ex-date	Apple return (%)	Path of wealth – POW	Average return (%)	POW from average returns
3/1/2017	139.79	2.044		2.044	120.87	0.469	120.00
3/2/2017	138.96	−0.594		−0.594	120.15	0.469	120.56
3/3/2017	139.78	0.590		0.590	120.86	0.469	121.13
Arithmetic average return				0.469			
Geometric average return					0.452%		

definition of the return on a security between two dates, t and t − 1.

$$R_t = [(P_t - P_{t-1}) + \text{Cash Payout}_t]/P_{t-1}. \qquad (1.1)$$

If the security in question were a stock, the cash payout would be the dividend and it would be added on the ex-date, but Eq. (1.1) holds for any security.

The fifth column of Exhibit 1.1 presents the sequence of returns on Apple stock. It differs from the percentage price change only in February 9, 2017, which was the ex-date. On that day, which is depicted in bold, the dividend is added to the change in price to compute the return, as shown in Eq. (1.1).

Once you have a series of returns it is possible to calculate one of the most important measures of investment performance, the path of wealth or POW. The POW shows the value of your investment from a given starting point, $100 in Exhibit 1.1. The calculation assumes that any dividends received are reinvested in the security in question – Apple stock in the exhibit. The POW is presented in the sixth column of Exhibit 1.1. It shows that an investor who invested $100 in Apple stock on January 3, 2017 would have an investment worth $120.86 as of the market close on March 3, 2017. It also shows the value of that initial $100 investment for each day in the two-month period.

Investment performance should always be assessed using returns and POWs, not price charts. The problem is that much financial performance data presented in the media are based on price charts, not POWs. This is true not only for individual stocks but also for the best-known indexes. For instance, neither the Dow Jones index nor the S&P 500 index takes account of dividends. Therefore, if you compare the performance, of say, a mutual fund you own with the S&P 500, you have an apples to oranges problem. Mutual fund performance data typically are based on returns, whereas the S&P 500 is a price index that excludes dividends. As a result, the performance of the portfolio of stocks that the S&P 500 is comprised of is significantly better than the price appreciation of the index because many stocks in the index pay dividends. The takeaway is that when comparing two investments you want to be sure to compare POWs. This is not often easy. For example, return data for the S&P 500 and Dow Jones index are not readily available.

It may seem like the dividend issue is a minor annoyance. In Exhibit 1.1, the dividend accounts for a minor part of the total return on Apple stock. But while stock prices move up and down, dividends are never negative. As the investment holding period grows, the impact of dividends becomes more evident. To appreciate the importance of dividends, take a look at Exhibit 1.2, which plots the POW for the U.S. stock market from 1926 to 2017, both including and excluding dividends.

Before interpreting the results, a word on the data. The POWs shown in Exhibit 1.2 are calculated using data from the Center for Research in Securities Prices (CRSP) at the University of Chicago. CRSP provides daily data on the returns for virtually all listed U.S.

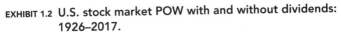

EXHIBIT 1.2 U.S. stock market POW with and without dividends: 1926–2017.

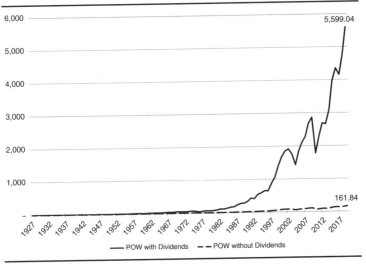

stocks back to 1926. What makes the CRSP data so convenient is that all the hard work of computing returns, such as adding dividends on the ex-date, has been done. CRSP also reports the market return, with and without dividends, for a value-weighted index of all listed stocks. As such, the CRSP index is far more comprehensive than the Dow, and even a good deal more comprehensive than the S&P 500. For that reason, it is used to measure market performance in most academic studies and, unless otherwise noted, when we refer to the market portfolio in this book, we mean the CRSP index.

Turning back to Exhibit 1.2, the results highlight the importance of accounting for dividends when calculating returns. The exhibit shows that an investment of $1 in the CRSP market portfolio in 1926 would be worth $5,599.04 if all dividends were reinvested along the way! If dividends are excluded, the value of the $1 investment grows only to $161.84 in 2017. This demonstrates that it is critical to properly include dividends, or other cash payouts, when computing POWs and not to be misled by price indexes.

Exhibit 1.2 should not be interpreted as saying that stocks that pay dividends offer higher returns than those that do not. The message simply is that if stocks do pay a dividend, it must be taken into account when computing the POW. With regard to comparing stocks that pay dividends versus those that do not, if we hold constant risk and taxes, there is no reason why the average long-run return should be different. Remember that the price of a stock tends to fall by the amount of the dividend on the ex-date. For stocks that do not pay dividends, there is no dividend but there is also no drop, so the return is unaffected. This is another reason to be sure to work with returns and not price changes.

As a further illustration of the utility of POWs, Exhibit 1.3 plots the POW for companies Coke, GE, IBM, and Amazon, along

EXHIBIT 1.3 POWs for a sample of companies: January 2000–July 2016.

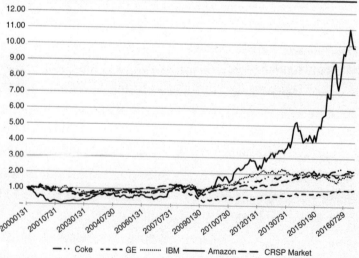

with the CRSP market index. The POWs are calculated using monthly return data from CRSP. One convenient feature of the CRSP data is that it provides monthly returns directly, avoiding the need to build them up from daily data. The exhibit shows that two of the companies, IBM and Coke, basically mirrored the market index while GE significantly underperformed and Amazon markedly outperformed.[1] Calculating POWs in this fashion is the proper way to compare the performance of various securities.

POWs can also be used to compare different measures of the market. Of the three market indexes we have discussed so far, the Dow is a particularly bad measure of the market because it contains only 30 stocks and because it is not calculated based on the market values of the constituent securities. Both the S&P 500 and the CRSP market index are good choices. They are both weighted by the value of the constituent securities. This means an investor could actually buy and hold both of these portfolios and match the index performance.[2] As noted previously, we will generally use the CRSP index in this book because it covers all securities traded on the New York, American, and NASDAQ markets stock exchanges.[3] Given this choice, a natural question to ask is: How much difference does the choice make when assessing market performance? Exhibit 1.4 answers the question.

The exhibit plots the POW using monthly data from 1926 to 2016 for both the S&P 500 and for the CRSP index. The main takeaway is that the two measures are very similar. Although the lines nearly overlap, they are not identical. Over the full period, the

---

[1] As interesting side note, famed investor Warren Buffett owned shares of IBM, Coke, and GE at times during the period, but never owned any shares of Amazon.
[2] The holding would have to be adjusted slightly to account for stocks leaving or entering the indexes.
[3] Since its acquisition by the New York Stock Exchange in 2009, the American Stock Exchange (AMEX) has been called the "NYSE Amex Equities."

EXHIBIT 1.4 **S&P 500 versus CRSP market index: 1926–2016.**

S&P 500 slightly outperforms the CRSP index. Therefore, when someone talks about the market, it is a good idea to ask them what they are talking about.

STOCKS, BONDS, AND BILLS

Calculation of POWs also makes it possible to compare the investment performance of various classes of investments. This is something we make use of throughout this book. As an initial example, Exhibit 1.5 compares what are probably the three most important classes of investments in securities – common stocks, long-term Treasury bonds, and short-term Treasury bills. Bonds and bills are described further in a subsequent chapter. For now, all you need to know is that they are obligations of the U.S. government that promise fixed future payments. The exhibit is

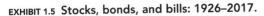

EXHIBIT 1.5 Stocks, bonds, and bills: 1926–2017.

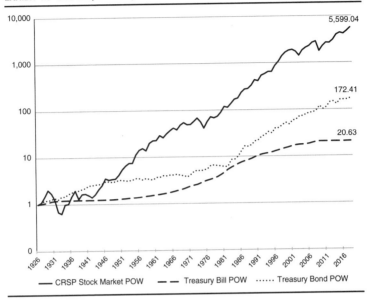

plotted on a logarithmic scale because the performances of the three asset classes are so different. For convenience, the return data underlying the POWs are reported in Exhibit 1.6. The exhibit underscores how what seem like relatively small differences in average returns translate into remarkably large differences in final wealth when compounded over 92 years. Whereas $1 invested in the CRSP index in 1926 grows to $5,599.04 in 2017, the same investment in Treasury bills grows only to $20.63. Treasury bonds are in the middle, with the $1 investment growing to $172.41.

A word to the wise. The vast performance differences between stocks, bonds, and bills is not something that one can automatically expect to continue going forward. What history says about what can be expected going forward is an issue we address in depth later in the book.

EXHIBIT 1.6 Return data for stocks, bonds, bills.

Date	CRSP stock market returns (%)	Treasury bill returns (%)	Treasury bond returns (%)	CRSP stock market POW	Treasury bill POW	Treasury bond POW
				1.00	1.00	1.00
1926	9.85	3.19	9.01	1.10	1.03	1.09
1927	32.87	3.12	11.33	1.46	1.06	1.21
1928	39.14	3.82	−0.52	2.03	1.10	1.21
1929	−15.10	4.74	6.12	1.72	1.16	1.28
1930	−28.90	2.35	6.76	1.23	1.18	1.37
1931	−44.39	1.02	−7.38	0.68	1.20	1.27
1932	−7.94	0.81	14.99	0.63	1.21	1.46
1933	57.41	0.29	1.20	0.99	1.21	1.47
1934	3.18	0.15	13.63	1.02	1.21	1.67
1935	45.45	0.17	6.95	1.48	1.21	1.79
1936	32.32	0.17	9.53	1.96	1.22	1.96
1937	−34.60	0.32	0.43	1.28	1.22	1.97
1938	28.44	0.04	6.78	1.65	1.22	2.10
1939	1.84	0.01	5.62	1.68	1.22	2.22
1940	−7.51	−0.06	12.37	1.55	1.22	2.50
1941	−10.04	0.04	1.48	1.40	1.22	2.53
1942	16.72	0.26	3.22	1.63	1.22	2.62
1943	27.97	0.34	2.08	2.09	1.23	2.67
1944	21.36	0.32	2.81	2.53	1.23	2.75
1945	39.06	0.32	10.73	3.52	1.24	3.04
1946	−6.42	0.35	−0.10	3.29	1.24	3.04
1947	3.29	0.46	−2.63	3.40	1.25	2.96
1948	2.13	0.98	3.40	3.47	1.26	3.06
1949	20.11	1.11	6.45	4.17	1.27	3.26
1950	30.47	1.21	0.06	5.45	1.29	3.26
1951	20.94	1.48	−3.94	6.59	1.31	3.13
1952	13.33	1.64	1.16	7.46	1.33	3.16
1953	0.38	1.78	3.63	7.49	1.35	3.28
1954	50.41	0.86	7.19	11.27	1.36	3.52
1955	25.41	1.56	−0.69	14.13	1.38	3.49
1956	8.58	2.42	−6.27	15.35	1.42	3.27
1957	−10.35	3.13	8.22	13.76	1.46	3.54
1958	44.78	1.42	−5.29	19.92	1.48	3.35
1959	12.65	2.82	−2.51	22.44	1.52	3.27
1960	1.21	2.58	13.32	22.71	1.56	3.71
1961	26.96	2.16	0.19	28.83	1.60	3.71
1962	−9.93	2.72	7.80	25.97	1.64	4.00
1963	21.40	3.15	−0.79	31.53	1.69	3.97
1964	16.35	3.52	4.11	36.68	1.75	4.13
1965	14.06	3.96	−0.27	41.84	1.82	4.12

EXHIBIT 1.6 (Continued)

Date	CRSP stock market returns (%)	Treasury bill returns (%)	Treasury bond returns (%)	CRSP stock market POW	Treasury bill POW	Treasury bond POW
1966	−8.86	4.71	3.96	38.13	1.91	4.29
1967	26.84	4.15	−6.02	48.36	1.99	4.03
1968	12.75	5.29	−1.20	54.53	2.09	3.98
1969	−9.82	6.59	−6.52	49.18	2.23	3.72
1970	1.29	6.38	12.69	49.81	2.37	4.19
1971	15.84	4.32	16.70	57.70	2.47	4.89
1972	17.64	3.89	5.15	67.88	2.57	5.14
1973	−16.92	7.06	−2.49	56.39	2.75	5.02
1974	−26.81	8.08	3.89	41.27	2.97	5.21
1975	37.66	5.82	6.10	56.82	3.15	5.53
1976	26.25	5.16	18.18	71.73	3.31	6.53
1977	−4.84	5.15	0.90	68.26	3.48	6.59
1978	7.33	7.31	−2.93	73.27	3.73	6.40
1979	21.88	10.69	−1.52	89.30	4.13	6.30
1980	32.63	11.52	−3.52	118.44	4.61	6.08
1981	−4.14	14.86	1.16	113.53	5.29	6.15
1982	21.00	10.66	39.74	137.37	5.86	8.60
1983	22.76	8.85	1.28	168.63	6.38	8.71
1984	5.79	9.96	15.81	178.39	7.01	10.08
1985	31.74	7.68	31.96	235.01	7.55	13.30
1986	17.32	6.06	25.79	275.72	8.01	16.73
1987	2.89	5.38	−2.91	283.69	8.44	16.25
1988	17.57	6.32	8.71	333.53	8.97	17.66
1989	29.61	8.22	19.23	432.29	9.71	21.06
1990	−4.27	7.68	6.15	413.85	10.46	22.35
1991	30.65	5.51	18.59	540.71	11.03	26.51
1992	8.22	3.40	7.95	585.14	11.41	28.62
1993	10.75	2.90	16.91	648.04	11.74	33.46
1994	−0.09	3.88	−7.19	647.47	12.19	31.05
1995	35.07	5.53	30.38	874.51	12.87	40.48
1996	21.35	5.14	−0.35	1061.19	13.53	40.34
1997	32.32	5.08	15.46	1404.13	14.22	46.58
1998	19.13	4.78	13.05	1672.80	14.90	52.66
1999	10.38	4.56	−8.66	1846.43	15.57	48.10
2000	3.47	5.76	20.95	1910.59	16.47	58.17
2001	−8.45	3.78	4.09	1749.15	17.09	60.55
2002	−18.22	1.63	17.22	1430.54	17.37	70.98
2003	29.13	1.02	2.45	1847.32	17.55	72.72
2004	13.88	1.20	8.28	2103.67	17.76	78.74
2005	8.45	2.96	7.66	2281.49	18.29	84.77
2006	17.62	4.79	1.14	2683.55	19.16	85.73

EXHIBIT 1.6 (Continued)

Date	CRSP stock market returns (%)	Treasury bill returns (%)	Treasury bond returns (%)	CRSP stock market POW	Treasury bill POW	Treasury bond POW
2007	6.62	4.67	9.74	2861.21	20.06	94.08
2008	−37.83	1.47	25.60	1778.89	20.35	118.16
2009	28.13	0.10	−13.99	2279.23	20.37	101.63
2010	17.78	0.12	9.77	2684.42	20.40	111.56
2011	−0.89	0.04	26.99	2660.65	20.41	141.68
2012	15.51	0.06	3.88	3073.41	20.42	147.18
2013	29.45	0.03	−12.23	3978.64	20.42	129.17
2014	9.45	0.02	24.62	4354.70	20.43	160.97
2015	−4.55	0.01	−0.67	4156.62	20.43	159.89
2016	14.48	0.19	1.38	4758.33	20.47	162.10
2017	17.67	0.79	6.36	5599.04	20.63	172.41
Average	11.69	3.39	6.19			
Volatility	19.48	3.14	9.88			

RETURN MATHEMATICS

Although daily returns are the "atoms" of investment analysis, they are rarely reported as such. It is more common, for instance, to report returns in annual terms. This requires doing the math to convert from one interval to another. The basic formula that does that is

$$W_n = W_0 * (1 + r_1) * (1 + r_2) * (1 + r_3) * \cdots (1 + r_n) \quad (1.2)$$

where W_0 is the initial wealth invested, r_i is the return on day i, n is the total number of trading days the investment is held, and W_n is the final value of the investment.[4] Equation (1.2) is what was used to construct the POW – each trading day W_n is incremented by one day.

---

[4] Equation (1.2) is cumbersome because the returns compound rather than adding. There is a way around this complexity by using continuously compounded returns rather than standard returns. While continuous returns are often used in academic studies, standard returns remain the norm in almost all practical investment publications. Therefore, we use standard returns in this book. A detailed discussion of continuous returns can be found in any major investment textbook.

Equation (1.2) can also be used to compute returns over periods longer than one day. Suppose that you have a series of daily returns but need a series of weekly returns. Assuming that the week is five trading days long, weekly returns are calculated in two steps. First Eq. (1.2) is used to compute W_5 as

$$W_5 = W_0 * (1 + r_1) * (1 + r_2) * (1 + r_3) * (1 + r_4) * (1 + r_5).$$

Next, the weekly return is defined by the equation

$$W_5 = W_0 * (1 + r_{weekly}).$$

So that,

$$r_{weekly} = w_5/w_0 - 1.$$

There is nothing unique about the weekly return. Monthly or annual returns can be calculated in the same way, though the calculation is a bit cumbersome. A common calculation is converting monthly returns to annual returns using the formula,

$$r_{annual} = (1 + r_{monthly})^{12} - 1. \qquad (1.3)$$

In Eq. (1.3), the two-step procedure has been telescoped into one step.

Converting returns between various intervals can be a pain, because weeks and months do not always have the same number of trading days. Fortunately, sophisticated data sources like CRSP have already done the work. As well as providing daily return data, these sources allow for the downloading of monthly returns or annual returns directly.

A final word of caution: in the financial media conversions of returns from one interval to another are not always done using the compounding formulas described above. It is common, for instance, to multiply a monthly return by 12 to get an annual return. This is an error because it excludes the benefits that accrue from reinvestment of returns earned earlier in the period. Taking account of reinvestment, a return of 1% per month is properly converted to an annual return of 12.68% per year, not 12%.

VOLATILITY

Thus far, we have focused on the level of returns. However, their variability is also important. Return variability is typically called volatility in finance and is calculated as the standard deviation of a sequence of returns.

To give a visual feel for volatility, Exhibit 1.7 plots the annual returns for the CRSP stock market index and Treasury bills over the period from 1926 to 2017. The difference between the two series is immediately obvious. The Treasury bill returns are typically small and often close to zero, the only exception being the high-inflation

EXHIBIT 1.7 CRSP market versus Treasury bill returns: 1926–2017.

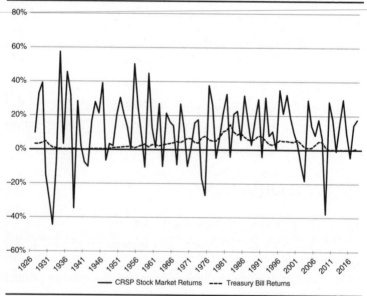

period of the late 1970s and early 1980s (an issue we will discuss in the chapter on inflation). More importantly, from the standpoint of volatility and risk, the Treasury bill returns are never negative. The CRSP market returns are dramatically different. Increases of around 40% occur in several years as do drops of 30%.[5]

Exhibit 1.7 also allows one to get a feeling for what finance professionals call "excess returns." Excess returns are the return on an investment minus the return on short-term Treasury bills. Excess returns can be thought of as a payment for bearing risk. We will discuss risk and return in much greater detail in Chapter 4. For now, notice that because Treasury bill returns are small and positive in every year and stock market returns have huge swings, there is not much difference between the return on stocks and the excess return in any individual year.

The bottom of Exhibit 1.6 shows that the volatility of the market index is 19.5% per year. The average return is 11.7%. This means that a 95% confidence interval constructed around the average return would run all the way from −25.3% to 48.7%! In contrast, the average return on Treasury bills is 3.4% and the volatility is only 3.1%. This suggests that there is a risk–return trade-off with volatility as the measure of risk. The suggestion carries a kernel of truth, but only a kernel. The actual trade-off between risk and return is a good deal more complex. We address the risk–return trade-off in detail in Chapter 4.

AVERAGE RETURNS

Because returns vary day to day, it is often useful to calculate the average return on an investment. For instance, suppose you buy

---

[5]Note that for the compounding calculations, the combination of a 40% increase and a 30% drop actually results in a 2% decline in the market.

IBM and Apple stock on the same day and would like to compare the average return on the two investments. It turns out that calculating the average is not as straightforward as you would hope. Turning back to Exhibit 1.1, the bottom of the fifth column that shows the Apple average return is 0.469%. More formally, this is known as the arithmetic average, but it is just the standard average with which you are familiar. It is calculated by dividing the sum of the returns by the number of returns.

It turns out that the standard arithmetic average has a peculiar property. To illustrate the problem, the average return is copied to all the cells in column seven. Next, a new POW is computed using the average return. That POW is reported in column eight. The problem is that the new POW shown in column eight is not equal to the original POW in column six. By the end of the period, the value of the investment has grown to \$121.13 instead of \$120.86.

There is nothing special about the Apple example. The ending value of the POW computed using the arithmetic average return will always exceed the actual ending POW unless all the returns are the same. Because of this anomaly, average returns are also computed using a procedure that ensures the ending POW values will be the same. This done by working with Eq. (1.2). The procedure for calculating the average begins by writing down the ending value calculated using actual series of investment returns as shown in Eq. (1.4)

$$W_n = W_0 * (1 + r_1) * (1 + r_2) * \cdots (1 + r_n) = W_0 * (1 + r_{av})^n$$
$$(1.4)$$

Equation (1.4) is then used to define the geometric average return, r_{av}, as that return that if earned and compounded every period produces the same ending value as the actual series of returns. Solving Eq. (1.4) for r_{av} gives,

$$r_{av} = (W_n/W_0)^{(1/n)} - 1 \qquad (1.5)$$

Applying Eq. (1.5) to the Apple returns gives a geometric average return of 0.452%. The geometric average is less than the arithmetic average, as it has to be because earning the arithmetic average led to a final value that exceeded the actual final value. It turns out that the difference between the geometric average and the arithmetic average depends on the variability of the series of returns. The more variable the returns, the greater this difference will be. But the geometric average is always less than the arithmetic average unless the returns are constant.

The foregoing should serve as a warning. Investors who hear that the average return on an investment was so and so should be careful. If it is not clear how the average was calculated, ask. To illustrate the mischief that can occur recall that the POW computed for the market showed that between 1926 and 2017 an investment of $1 grew to $5,599.04. During that time the arithmetic average return on the market as 11.69%. If the arithmetic average return is compounded for 92 years, it implies that an investment of $1 would have grown to $26,140.55 – almost five times the actual amount. This discrepancy highlights the importance of knowing how averages work.

Finally, returns can be computed for any asset as long as you have periodic data on prices and payouts. The Treasury bill return series used above is an example. But be aware that returns are often reported on assets like real estate for which periodic price data are not available. Under such circumstances, be sure to check what was used in the place of market prices when calculating returns. In the case of real estate, returns are often computed using periodic appraisals. But that means the return data are only as accurate as the appraisals.

USING RETURNS TO TEST INVESTMENT THEORIES

Suppose you read that internet stocks outperform utility stocks because they are more volatile. How do you tell if that is true? Before that question can even be addressed it must be translated into a testable hypothesis – that means it must be expressed in the language of returns. In terms of returns, the statement says that the average return and the average standard deviation of returns are both higher for internet stocks than they are for utility stocks. When stated this way, it becomes a testable hypothesis. Whether the test is meaningful and whether a positive finding implies causality are tricky issues, but that is not the point here. The point is that for statements about investments to have meaningful, testable content, they must be expressed in terms of returns.

As we write this, concern has been expressed in the financial press that if inflation were to accelerate suddenly it would be bad news for the stock market. If that concern is valid, then it should be the case that previous bouts of unexpected inflation were associated with market returns below the long run average. Now that the concern has been translated into a statement about returns, it can be tested. Once again, we do not want to overplay the importance of the particular suggested test. The relation between inflation and the stock market may be more complicated than that. But however complicated it may be, the relation does not become meaningful and testable until it is stated in terms of returns.

What goes for the two simple examples above is true of the most sophisticated academic theories of asset pricing. They are all stated and tested in terms of returns.

The bottom line is you cannot begin to analyze investments until you are comfortable calculating and working with returns. Fortunately, modern spreadsheet software makes it relatively easy to perform the necessary calculations. In addition, the requisite data to construct sequences of returns and POWs is freely available at both Google Finance and Yahoo Finance. To help you in your efforts, the data used in constructing the exhibits is available at www.wiley.com/go/CornellCFOI (Password: CFI).

RETURNS AND STOCK MARKET HISTORY

The sequence of past returns is the best summary of stock market history. If there is some pattern to the market, it must be discernable in the history of returns. Consider, for instance, technical analysis. Technical analysts construct all sorts of complicated charts that they suggest give insight into where the market is going in the future. Those charts are just a way of summarizing return data, akin to the POWs. If there is a predictable pattern that can be discerned with charts and used to predict future performance, it must be there in the history of returns. This fact has not been lost on generations of graduate students. With continually improving computer technology and ever more complete financial data, they have been combing through return data for every single stock as well as market indexes, down to second-to-second trades, in an attempt to find patterns. In the last 50 years, thousands of papers have been published on the issue and there are undoubtedly thousands more that never got over the publication hurdle.

The basic message is that there are no patterns in stock prices – at least none that can be reliably exploited to earn superior risk-adjusted returns. To be fair there is on ongoing dispute about this issue that involves the question of data mining. We analyze data mining in more detail in Chapter 7. To anticipate that discussion, the issue raised by data mining is that even random series have quirks that look like exploitable patterns. If enough people pore over the same data, they will find those quirks, but the quirks will have no meaning. The dispute is over whether the quirks that have been found are meaningful. Nonetheless, virtually all researchers agree that in the case of stock market data even these quirks are few and far between.

Of course, it is possible that there are relationships that have been overlooked. If you think you have found an exception, the way to test it is using returns. For example, one of the earliest tests involved what is called autocorrelation. Some analysts believed that big positive returns tended to be followed by additional positive returns and vice-versa for negative returns. To a statistician this means that returns are positively autocorrelated. Tests for positive autocorrelation are easy to run and the answer, almost invariably, is that there is no meaningful autocorrelation. What you want to be careful to avoid is ad hoc theorizing based on a few observations. Any alleged pattern worth risking money on is worth testing carefully. And with the return data available today that is not hard. We will revisit to this issue in future chapters.

CONCEPTUAL FOUNDATION 1

The first conceptual foundation of investing is that returns are the fundamental unit of investment analysis. Investment performance should always be measured using a combination of return data and paths of wealth. Before any theory about stock market behavior can be tested, it must first be translated into the language of returns. In later chapters, when we turn to topics such as inflation and the risk–return trade-off, returns will be at the center of the discussion.

2

THE ECONOMIC STRUCTURE OF INVESTMENT MARKETS

A typical major league pitcher throws a fastball at 95 miles per hour or 42.47 meters per second. Ignoring air resistance, if you were to drop a baseball from a building how high would the building have to be for the ball to be traveling at 95 miles per hour when it hits the ground?

This is what we call a game against nature. The task is to find the rules by which nature operates and apply them to solve the problem. In this case, Isaac Newton has already solved the problem and the answer is 92.1 m or 302.2 ft.[1] Once the problem has been

---

[1] The problem can be solved by applying the law of conservation of energy. Setting the potential energy at the start, mgh, equal to the kinetic energy, $(1/2)mv^2$, at the end and solving for h.

solved, the nice thing is that it always works. It does not matter whether you drop the ball today, tomorrow, or next week. If the building is 302.2 ft. tall, the ball always hits the ground at 95 miles per hour. In fact, the law held even before Isaac Newton was born. Nature does not care if we know her laws or not. She follows them one way or the other.

Now consider a soccer player facing a crucial penalty kick. What is the best place to kick the ball? High? Low? Left? Right? While there might be a best answer in one particular instance, there is no general, timeless, solution to the problem. If the answer was always high right, the goalie would move to the right and be ready to jump. But if the goalie did that, the answer would now be low left. This is a game against an intelligent agent and it has no static solution – there is not a best place to kick the ball.

Games against markets are of the second type. There cannot be simple, unvarying rules that makes it possible to beat the market because if there were, they would eventually be widely adopted and, thereby, cease to work. We call this the Catch-22 of investing: *Any investment rule that can be clearly articulated and easily applied is one that won't work.*

This may strike you as an overly strong statement. It seems like the science of finance should be able to identify superior companies. That depends on what is meant by "superior." If it means companies with better earnings prospects, the answer is yes. It is not difficult to discern that Amazon has better financial prospects than Target. But if it means companies that are better investments, the answer is basically, no. The reason is that the quality of an investment depends on price as well as on a company's prospects. No matter how good a company's financial outlook, at some price it becomes a bad investment. For instance, at the hedge fund we run, which goes by the initials SMBP, we think Amazon is a wonderful company, but at a price of nearly $1700 per share we do not think it is a particularly good investment. The problem with much investment analysis is that it fails to pay enough attention to price. An analyst might go on and on about Amazon's software, web services, delivery systems, potential to disrupt new markets, and so forth without asking the critical question: To what extent does the market price already reflect those characteristics? If it does already reflect them, then all those wonderful attributes are no reason to hold an over-weighted position in the stock.

It is the role of price that makes investing a game against other intelligent agents, not a game against nature. As we will develop in detail in the next section, whenever you buy a security someone else is selling. If there were a simple investment rule that said, "now is the time to buy," who would be the seller? Presumably potential sellers would refrain from selling until the price had risen sufficiently such that the rule said it was no longer the time to buy.

The importance of price also implies that what it means to "beat the market" must be defined in terms of returns, because returns take account of the current price of an investment. Therefore, finance theory defines beating the market as earning a *risk-adjusted* rate of return over the long run that exceeds the return market portfolio. The answer sounds good, but it is vacuous without a specification of how the risk adjustment is to be done. That turns out to be the subject of a massive ongoing debate in finance that we will return to throughout this book. For now, take it as a matter of faith that the risk adjustment can be done, so it makes sense to use the phrase "beat the market."

THE ARITHMETIC OF FINANCIAL MARKETS

The arithmetic of financial markets begins with the recognition that all securities must be held by investors. For the time being, let's focus on stocks, although the same analysis can be applied to other securities markets as well. If we consider all investors as an aggregate group, then that group by definition holds all the stocks. Stocks can move from one investor to another within the group, but like a hot potato they can only be exchanged, not created or destroyed.[2]

The fact that stocks must be held has important implications for the arithmetic of investment performance, as demonstrated by Nobel Prize winner William Sharpe. Prof. Sharpe's analysis can be best illustrated by considering an example in which stock market investors can be divided into two groups: passive investors, who simply hold the market portfolio, and active investors, encompassing everyone else. It is worth pausing for a moment to more fully explain Sharpe's definition of active investors. It is not limited to investors who trade actively, though they would be included in the group. It literally includes all investors who hold portfolios that deviate from the aggregate market. Notice that by this definition Warren Buffett is a very active investor. Although he does not trade much, he says his ideal holding period is forever, his holdings are concentrated in relatively few stocks. Consequently, his portfolio diverges significantly from the market portfolio.

Given this framework, assume that in a given year the market return is 10% (it could be any number). The passive investors earn 10% by definition because they are holding the market portfolio. But if the market return is 10%, and the passive investors' return is

---

[2]Actually, the statement is an approximation. If account is taken of buybacks and new issues by companies, then the amount of stock held by investors as a group can change. However, this is a second-order effect, which we ignore here.

10%, then the active investors, as a group, must also earn a return of 10%. There is no economics to this conclusion. It is an implication of arithmetic given the fact that all stocks must be held.

Unlike passive investors, active investors bear added costs. They employ PhDs, perform complex economic and statistical analysis, do extensive security analysis and valuation, pay the transactions costs of active trading, and so forth. On a net-of-cost basis, therefore, active investors as a group must always do worse than passive investors. In terms of the previous example, their net return will be less than 10%. The conclusion is sufficiently shocking that it bears repeating. Passive investors as a group will always outperform active investors as a group no matter what happens in the market place.

What is remarkable about Sharpe's analysis is what it does *not* assume. It does not assume that financial markets are competitive – they could be dominated by a few large institutions. It does not assume that investors are rational – they could be wildly emotional and trade on whims. It does not assume that information is widely distributed – there could be rampant insider trading. It does not depend on any assumptions about the nature of security returns. All that is required are the rules of arithmetic and the fact that all securities have to be held.

Some investors, on learning of Sharpe's analysis for the first time, think it simply cannot be true. What, for example, would happen if there was significant insider trading? To see what happens in the context of Sharpe's arithmetic, let's set aside any prohibitions against insider trading and consider a simple example. Suppose that GoPro, the action camera company, is trading at $8.00 and some connected investors are tipped that Apple is going to make an offer to buy the company at $12.00 next week. The tipped investors will clearly want to accumulate GoPro stock as long as they can buy it for less than $12.00, but how do they do that? They cannot buy from the passive investors, because they are holding the market portfolio. If the price of GoPro rises, so that it constitutes more of the market, they do not sell because they want to maintain their market allocation. Therefore, the tipped investors have to buy from other active investors. For instance, if the price of GoPro rises to $9.00, due to the activity of insiders, some active investors may conclude the stock is now overvalued and sell. There may also be active investors who no longer like the "chart action." Whatever the reason, the insiders can increase their holding above GoPro's pro rata share of the market portfolio only to the extent that other active investors are willing to hold less than GoPro's pro rata share. When the information comes out and the price rises to $12.00, the insiders benefit at the expense of the active investors who reduced their holdings. The passive investors get the *pro rata* market share of the price increase from $8.00 to $12.00. The passive investors cannot be exploited because they are not a counterparty to the informed trade.

What the example makes clear is that the only way for some active investors to escape the logic of Sharpe's arithmetic is at the expense of other active investors. If we divide active investors into two groups, winners and losers, the losers end up not only paying all the costs of active investing, they also have the losses associated with transferring wealth to the winners. Clearly, no active investor expects to be in the loser group *ex ante*, but just as clearly about half will be *ex post*.

From the standpoint of small and individual investors, Sharpe's arithmetic seems almost too good to be true. It is easy for such investors to be intimidated by the constant drumbeat regarding how technology is revolutionizing investing. There are stories about secretive mathematical geniuses behind firms like D.E.

Shaw and Renaissance Technologies that manage tens of billions of dollars using proprietary computer technology. Michael Lewis's best-selling book *Flash Boys* recounts the activities of high-frequency traders who measure trading times in milliseconds. Connected investors like George Soros meet with leading executives and politicians in exotic places like Davos, Switzerland to discuss the future of the world economy and what it means for their portfolio. And none of that matters. A small investor who is passive will still outperform the pool of active investors, which includes all those connected geniuses. The only way those savvy traders can beat the market is at the expense of other active investors.

In this respect, Sharpe's arithmetic also comes with a warning. As soon as you deviate from the market portfolio, you are an active investor. That means you are running the risk of being a counterparty to trades by Berkshire Hathaway or Goldman Sachs. For instance, assume that you have concluded the GE's price drop in 2017 was overdone and that the stock appears to be underpriced. As a result, you want to hold more GE in your portfolio than its approximate weight of 0.46% in the Center for Research in Securities Prices (CRSP) index. As soon as you increase your holding beyond GE's market weight, you have become an active investor. In order for you to hold more of GE's pro rata share of the market, some active counterparties have to hold less than that fraction in GE. It behooves you to ask who those counterparties might be and why you think your analysis is better than theirs.

Finally, the Sharpe arithmetic applies not only to the market as a whole, but to all subsectors. Consider, for instance, investment in technology stocks. An investor who passively holds an index of such stocks will outperform the average active investor who trades them.

To conclude, we feel that the importance of Sharpe's analysis cannot be overstated. If there is one thing every investor should know, it is the arithmetic of financial markets. The logic is inescapable and the implications are broad. It should be the starting point of any investment analysis.

THE EFFICIENT MARKET HYPOTHESIS

The arithmetic of financial markets is easy to confuse with the efficient market hypothesis (EMH). The best way to understand the EMH is to move away from the complexity of the stock market and consider the market for betting on football games. In the football betting market the analog to a security price is the point spread. Point spreads determine how much you must "pay" to bet on the team of your choice. For example, the point spread prior to the 2017 Super Bowl was "New England plus three." This spread means that a bet on the New England Patriots pays off only if the Patriots win by four or more. If the Patriots win by three points, the bet is a tie and all moneys are returned. If the Patriots win by two points or less, or if they lose the game, the bet is lost.

To see how the point spread is analogous to the price of a security, imagine an investor who has decided that the Patriots are a better team and thinks that the Patriots should win by seven points. At spreads of "New England plus three" or at "New England plus four" this hypothetical investor will bet on the Patriots. However, at a spread of "New England plus nine" the cost of betting on the Patriots is so high that the hypothetical investor will switch sides and bet on the Atlanta Falcons. In a market made up of thousands of such investors, the number betting on the Patriots falls as the point spread rises in the same fashion as the number of investors willing to buy IBM stock falls as the stock price rises.

Like stock prices, point spreads are determined by the law of supply and demand operating through a network of brokers (called bookmakers) with whom investors place their bets. The bookmakers earn their money by charging a small "commission" on every bet. The commission, commonly referred to as "vigorish," is typically 5%. It is collected by requiring the loser to pay $110 for every $100 bet while the winner collects only $100. As long as equal amounts are bet on each team the bookmakers earn their commission no matter who wins and thus bear no risk.[3] To assure that equal amounts are bet on each team the bookmakers adjust the point spread. If more money is being bet on the Patriots than on the Falcons at New England plus three, the spread is raised to New England plus four. By adjusting the point spread, the bookmakers balance the amount bet on each team in the same fashion as the specialist on the floor of the New York Stock Exchange balances buy and sell orders for IBM stock by adjusting the price. When supply equals demand, that is when equal amounts are being bet on each team, the market is in "equilibrium."

The extent to which a gambler influences the market price (point spread) depends on the amount he or she is willing to bet. The more confident a gambler is in his or her selection, the more he or she will bet and the greater will be his or her impact on the point spread. In equating supply and demand, the market aggregates the opinions of all investors, weighted by the amount they are willing to bet, to arrive at an average "opinion." This average, or market, opinion is represented by the equilibrium point spread. Prior to the 2017 Super Bowl, the market opinion was that the New England Patriots were three points better than the Atlanta Falcons.

Though the equilibrium point spread reflects the average opinion, the average is not a consensus. In fact, if everyone agreed that

---

[3]Active football gamblers may recognize that bookmakers typically bear some risk even when equal amounts are bet on each team because not all bets are placed at the same point spread.

the appropriate point spread was New England plus three, no one would bet on the game. Clearly, those betting on New England feel the equilibrium point spread is too low, while those betting on Atlanta think the equilibrium spread is too high.

Because the equilibrium point spread is an average of the opinions of all the investors who bet on a game, weighted by the amount they are willing to bet, anything that alters investor opinions will affect the point spread. Suppose, for instance, that two days prior to the 2017 Super Bowl the Patriots' star quarterback, Tom Brady, is injured. As soon as this information is released, investor estimates of the outcome of the game will change. At New England plus three some people who had originally planned to bet on the Patriots would now bet on the Falcons instead. As a result, supply no longer equals demand at the plus three point spread. Consequently, bookmakers would adjust the point spread until equal amounts are being bet on each team once again. To continue the illustration, assume that the new equilibrium point spread is New England minus three.

The change in the point spread from three to minus three demonstrates the sense in which market prices can be said to incorporate, or reflect, new information. Prior to Mr. Brady's injury the equilibrium point spread was New England plus three. Following his injury the equilibrium spread was New England minus three. Thus the information regarding Mr. Brady's injury was worth six points. The spread moves from plus three to minus three to "reflect" the new information.

In the case of IBM stock, the analog to betting on the Falcons or Patriots is deciding whether to buy or sell the stock. Whereas the point spread averages opinions about football teams, the stock price averages opinions about IBM. For IBM to sell at $170 per share, the number of shares of IBM that investors want to hold at that price must equal the number of IBM shares outstanding.

Furthermore, stock prices respond to new information in the same fashion as the point spread does. If IBM announces an unexpected drop in earnings, supply and demand will no longer be equal at the previous market price. To bring the market back into equilibrium, the price must fall.

The football betting analogy makes it easy to understand the concept of an efficient market. According to the most widely accepted definition, *an efficient market is a market in which the price of a security reflects all publicly available information.* In the context of the football betting market, the EMH says that the point spread reflects all publicly available information about the relative abilities of the two teams. In the case of the stock market, the EMH says that the market price of a security reflects publicly available information regarding the value of the security.

It is important to distinguish market efficiency from market clairvoyance. The EMH maintains that the market processes publicly available information as well as any professional investor does; it does not say that the market processes information perfectly or that it can predict the future without error. This is clear in the context of the football betting market. The market came close to its prediction of a three-point Patriots' victory in the 2017 Super Bowl, when the Patriots went on to win by six. The market was far less accurate in the 2007 Super Bowl when the Patriots lost to the New York Giants by three points despite being 12-point favorites. The same is true in the case of the stock market. Highly valued companies on occasion have performed hideously, to the surprise of many. The EMH recognizes that both markets and well-informed investors will make mistakes, but it predicts that, on average, market forecasts and market valuations will be at least as accurate as those produced by investors, no matter how expert.

The EMH implies that without inside information, investors, on average, cannot beat the market. If security prices properly reflect all public information, there are no underpriced or overpriced securities that can be discerned on the basis of that information. But saying that all securities are fairly priced is the same thing as saying that investors who buy those securities will only earn a fair, risk-adjusted, return on the investment.

Famous successful investors like Charlie Munger like to make fun of the EMH and the professors who they claim are its adherents. Ironically, since the early 1980s academics have been saying that the EMH cannot possibly be true. Markets do not become efficient because of the operation of some mysterious force like dark energy. Rather, they become efficient because investors do the hard work. Investor pore through financial statements, attend company presentations, analyze company products, study stock market history, and so on. All of these activities cost money. If the market was fully efficient, so that investors could not earn a fair return on the time and funds required to do investment research, they would stop doing it. But if investors stopped doing research, prices would tend to diverge from fair value. The result is that in equilibrium the market must be sufficiently inefficient that savvy investors can earn a fair rate of return on their investment in research. Consequently, the best description of the current academic viewpoint is that financial markets are highly competitive, but not fully efficient.

INFORMATIONAL VERSUS FUNDAMENTAL MARKET EFFICIENCY

If financial markets cannot be fully efficient, how efficient are they? That proves to be a very hard question to answer. After 50 years of research, the best answer remains, "we don't know," but there is a caveat. That caveat involves distinguishing between what is called informational efficiency and fundamental efficiency.

A market is said to be informationally efficient if it responds quickly to significant new information. The evidence in favor of informational efficiency of financial markets is overwhelming. A prime example is the response to earnings announcements. When a company either exceeds or falls short of expected earnings by a meaningful amount, the company's stock price typically responds within seconds. Such quick responses are not limited to company-specific news. Major macroeconomic announcements such as a sharp unexpected movement in inflation have an immediate impact on stock prices. The same is true of unexpected political events such as 9/11.

But fast response to information is not the same thing as a fundamentally correct response to information. A company's stock price may move in response to an earning miss, but did it move the right amount? More importantly, was the initial stock price before the movement reflective of the fundamental value of the company? These questions relate to the concept of fundamental efficiency – do stock markets rationally reflect a company's fundamental value? The fair answer here is that we simply do not know.

The reason for our ignorance was laid out in a classic article by Larry Summers in 1986. To use his own words, what Summers showed was that

> *Existing evidence does not establish that financial markets are efficient in the sense of rationally reflecting fundamentals … the types of statistical tests which have been used to date have essentially no power against at least one interesting alternative hypothesis to market efficiency. Thus the inability of these tests to reject market*

efficiency does not mean that they provide evidence in favor of its acceptance. In particular, the data in conjunction with current methods provide no evidence against the view that financial market prices deviate widely and frequently from rational valuations.

To offer one specific example to illustrate the distinction. Tesla is a company of intense interest to investors. The price of Tesla is so sensitive to news that it reacts to the slightest hint of information. Tesla is one of the most informationally efficient stocks in the world. Does that mean that the price reflects fundamental value? At SMBP we think it does not, but that is just our opinion. What Summers shows is that the hypersensitivity to information could be maintained even if the market price of the stock were half of or twice its fundamental value.

That brings to mind a statement made by Fischer Black in his Presidential address to the American Finance Association.[4] Black stated that,

All estimates of value are noisy, so we can never know how far away price is from value. However, we might define an efficient market as one in which price is within a factor of 2 of value, i.e., the price is more than half of value and less than twice value. The factor of 2 is arbitrary, of course. Intuitively, though, it seems reasonable to me, in the light of sources of uncertainty about value and the strength of the forces tending to cause price to return to value. By this definition, I think almost all markets are efficient almost all of the time. "Almost all" means at least 90%.

---

[4] Only his premature death prevented Fischer Black from winning the Nobel Prize for his path-breaking work on the theory of option pricing.

Black's view is consistent with that of Summers and with the research that been done in the 30 years since they made their comments. The prevailing view remains that while prices respond quickly to news, there is insufficient evidence to conclude that they rationally reflect fundamental value. If anything, the rise of behavioral finance has cast further doubt on the hypothesis of fundamental efficiency. To this day, the extent to which stock markets are fundamentally efficient remains an unanswered question. That opens the door to the view that active trading based on fundamental valuation may provide superior returns. But the fact that the door is open does not mean that any specific investor should walk through it. If market price diverges from fundamental value, the discrepancy between fundamental value and the value estimated by a particular investor may be even greater. To beat the market, it must not only be the case that the market makes mistakes, it must also be the case that the investor in question makes fewer.

It may seem like the foregoing is contradictory. If prices can diverge significantly from fundamental value shouldn't it be easy to make superior returns based on assessment of fundamental value? There are a number of reasons why this is not the case. The first is that "fundamental value" is not observable. As with the example of Tesla and SMBP, fundamental value is a matter of opinion and opinions can be wrong. Second, even if the investor measures fundamental value properly, there is no reason to believe that the market will converge to it any time soon. If the market is making a mistake today, it is likely to make the same mistake tomorrow. In fact, the error can even grow over time, leading to short-term losses for the fundamental investor. Third, stock prices are highly variable. To make superior returns based on an assessment of fundamental value, an investor must overweight the undervalued stocks (relative to their weight in the market portfolio) and decrease the holdings (or even short) of overvalued stocks. Doing so involves bearing added risk, as we discuss in Chapter 4 on risk and return. Finally, although markets not perfectly efficient, they are highly competitive. If there were an unambiguous way to identify mispriced stocks, savvy investors would immediately take advantage of that and prices would move quickly to eliminate the mispricing. As a result, in a competitive market the only examples of mispricing that will persist are those that are hard to identify and difficult to exploit.

This does not mean that superior investing based on fundamental valuation is doomed to fail. For instance, Warren Buffett is a fundamental investor and can hardly be called a failure. It does mean, however, that the task is a difficult one that is fraught with risk. This is an issue we examine further in Chapter 5.

To conclude, Larry Summers offers an insightful analogy related to "ketchup economics." He observes that in one sense the ketchup market is highly efficient in that two-quart bottles of ketchup invariably sell for twice as much as one-quart bottles of ketchup except for deviations traceable to transaction costs. He stresses, however, that this does not mean that the fundamental price of ketchup is correct. Also, the fact that any deviation of the price of two-quart bottles from twice the price of one-quart bottles is quickly arbitraged away does not mean that if the price of ketchup generally deviates from fundamental value there is an equally strong force driving it back toward equilibrium.

THE EFFICIENT MARKET HYPOTHESIS AND SHARPE'S ARITHMETIC

The EMH may appear to be a restatement of Sharpe's arithmetic, but there is a subtle and important difference. Sharpe's arithmetic does not say anything about security pricing or market efficiency. The market could be wildly inefficient and subject to waves of emotion that produce consistent mispricing and the conclusions of Sharpe's arithmetic would still hold. Passive investors would still out perform active investors as a group. If active investors are to take advantage of mispricing, it must be at the expense of other active investors who are unaware of the mispricing. The EMH makes a much stronger statement. In an efficient market, there are no mispriced securities based on publicly available information so *none* of the active investors can consistently beat the market. This is actually good news for bad active investors because if all securities are fairly priced there is no way for the sophisticated active traders to exploit the naïve ones.

This point is worth pursuing further. The EMH is often presented as a reason that investors should be passive. For instance, a leading fund manager in his memo to clients stated that, "the wisdom of passive investing stems from the belief that the effort of active investors causes assets to be fairly priced – that's why there are no bargains to be found." The manager is correct that if the EMH holds, investors should be passive because research and trading produce costs without benefits. But as we just showed, markets cannot be that efficient in equilibrium. Does that mean that investors should be active, or pay for active managers? No, the converse does not follow. Even in highly inefficient markets, there is a strong argument for passive investing – Bill Sharpe's arithmetic. In fact, in highly inefficient markets it is probably more important for individual investors to be passive. The reason is that they are likely to become counterparties to the trades that allow the more sophisticated investors to beat the market. The greater the potential mispricing, the more likely it is that naïve investors will end up on the wrong side of trades involving those mispriced securities. To be more specific, assume that there are a number of significantly overpriced and underpriced securities. If an individual investor is passive, he or she will hold both in proportion to the market shares. The result will be an offset. However, if that individual investor is active, he or she is likely to end up holding an over-weighted fraction of the overpriced securities and an under-weighted fraction of the underpriced securities. The net result will be poor investment performance. In fact, academic research finds that individual investors underperform passive indexes. In terms of the Sharpe arithmetic, they are the underperforming active investors who make it possible for more sophisticated active investors to earn superior returns.

Individual investors can totally eliminate the risk of such under-performance, and be assured of outperforming the average active investor, by passively holding an index fund that tracks the market portfolio. This is why it is so important for individual investors to understand Bill Sharpe's arithmetic and to appreciate the fact that it holds whether or not the market is efficient. It also raises another question that every investor should ask: Who is my counterparty likely to be?

WHO ARE YOUR COUNTERPARTIES?

Suppose that despite all the foregoing you have decided to become an active investor. You are aware of Prof. Sharpe's arithmetic that says that for you to do better than a passive investor, another active investor has to do worse. Who then are the other investors? Ken French spelled that out in his Presidential address to the American Finance Association in 2008. A summary of his findings is reproduced in Exhibit 2.1. Those with an eye to detail may notice that the percentages sum to more than 100%. That is because there is some unavoidable overlap among the categories. Nonetheless, the

EXHIBIT 2.1 Holders of U.S. equities in percent.

	1980	2007
Direct household holdings (%)	47.9	21.5
Mutual funds (%)	5.1	33.5
Exchange Traded funds (%)	0.0	3.0
Hedge funds (%)	0.0	2.2
Pension plans and ESOPs (%)	24.8	15.1
Public funds and non-profits (%)	12.7	12.9
Banks and insurance companies (%)	9.4	11.8
Foreign investors (%)	7.6	16.3

exhibit provides an excellent overview of the relative importance of different holders of U.S. equities.

The first thing to note in the exhibit is the marked decline in direct holdings by households from 47.9% of the total in 1980 to 21.5% in 2007. Furthermore, those numbers overstate the importance of what you might think of as "individual investors." A substantial fraction of the direct holdings is accounted for by very wealthy individuals like Warren Buffett and family corporations such as that run by the Pritzkers.

Second, exchange traded funds (ETFs) and hedge funds emerge. They account for none of the holdings in 1980. By 2007, they comprise over 5% of the total. Since 2008 their growth has been explosive, particularly for ETFs, so the data in the exhibit significantly understate those funds' current holdings. ETFs are also ideal vehicles for passive or quasi-passive investors. For instance, the Vanguard Group, the world's largest investment manager, has dozens of highly liquid ETFs, some with hundreds of billions under management. These funds do an excellent job of tracking well known indexes, including the S&P 500 and the CRSP total market index, at costs less than 0.10%, or 10 basis points, per year.[5] This makes well-diversified passive investment both easy and cost effective.

---

[5]A basis point is 1/100 of a percentage point.

Third, foreign holdings more than doubled from 7.6% in 1980 to 16.3% in 2007. Much of that increase was due to the rise of sophisticated sovereign wealth funds. For instance, the Norwegian sovereign wealth fund recently passed $1 trillion. It is widely considered to be one of the best managed funds in the world. China and Saudi Arabia also have immense sovereign wealth funds.

Fourth, mutual fund holdings jumped dramatically from 5.1% in 1980 to 33.5% in 2007. By 2007, mutual funds had replaced direct holders as the largest owners of U.S. equities.

Fifth, although pension holdings dropped from 24.8% of the total in 1980 to 15.1% in 2007, they remain substantial.

Sixth, public funds and non-profits remained stable at just over 12% of the total. However, this hides a shift, with public funds almost doubling and non-profits falling.

Finally, the holdings of banks and insurance companies remained largely constant at around 10%.

In the years since the publication of Prof. French's work, the main transformation has been the movement of investments from direct holdings to mutual funds and ETFs. Nonetheless, the overall picture remains the same. The market remains dominated, even more so than in 2007, by sophisticated institutional investors.

The institutions that appear in Exhibit 2.1 are final asset holders, but they often do not make the final investment decisions. For example, the California Public Employees Retirement System (CALPERS) is one of the largest public investors included in the exhibit. However, CALPERS does not manage their own money. Instead, they delegate the task to specialized money management firms such as the Capital Research and Management Company. To help them select those managers, asset owners also employ investment consulting firms, such as Wilshire Associates, which track and analyze the performance of the investment managers.

The foregoing implies that every time you trade, one of institutions shown in Exhibit 2.1, or its professional investment manager, is likely to be your counterparty. If you are buying because you think the stock is undervalued, you need to ask, "Why are they selling?" Remember, an active investor can beat the market only at the expense of another active investor. As we noted earlier, if your counterparty is Goldman Sachs or the Norwegian sovereign wealth funds, you need to ask, "What do you know that they don't?" It brings to mind an old joke about poker players that goes, "If you sit down to play cards and find yourself asking, 'Who is the sucker?', get up. You are the sucker." Prof. Sharpe's arithmetic is a clear warning that you might be the sucker. The implication is that you should trade sparingly with care and caution.

In attempting to heed this advice, the financial media are not helpful. Talking heads are constantly analyzing every minute announcement as if it has some trading implications. Many shows specialize in telling you what to buy or sell. Advertising wanders close to the line of deception. For example, one financial firm ran an ad showing a young man suffering in the back of an airplane. He wanders up toward first class and longingly stares at well-dressed people sitting on sofas and being offered wine by attractive flight attendants. Seeing him staring, one of the smiling flight attendants approaches, pauses, and closes the curtain in his face. Then the text appears on the screen, "Don't get mad, get eTrade." The implication is that once you start trading like a pro, you will be in first class. Prof. Sharpe would say that an inexperienced young man who becomes an active trader is likely to find Goldman Sachs or the like as a counterparty. Who do you think is going to beat the market? Remember, they both cannot.

There is also a continual flow of commentary regarding the irrationality of the market. Why, for example, would a rational market crash more than 20% in one day as it did in 1987? And why was there a flash crash in 2015? The implication is that if you are more rational than the market, you can beat the market. But as we discuss in the chapter on behavioral finance, even if many individual investors are emotional and irrational, it is unclear how that leads to profitable investment opportunities. Furthermore, the irrationality that infects the market might well be different from that which affects individuals. Most of the studies that document irrational behavior are done in university laboratories on individual college students. But Prof. French's work shows that investment decisions are not typically made by individuals, let alone college students. Instead they are made by institutions that employ professional managers specifically trained to make thoughtful, rational investment decisions. They may not always succeed in this endeavor, but what makes you think you will do better?

There is another, more subtle cost to active investing. Passive investors are generally well diversified. The most widely held passive portfolios simply match the S&P 500 or a total stock market index. Active investors, particularly individual active investors, are not so well diversified. The whole point of active investing is to overweight your portfolio in securities you believe are mispriced. This will not be all the stocks in the S&P 500. The problem, as we explain in the chapter on risk and return, is that risks that can be eliminated by diversification are not rewarded with risk premiums. Thus, active investors end up bearing uncompensated risk. This is OK if your security selection is good enough, but if you fail to pick winners, you end up bearing more risk with no benefit.

Perhaps the best way to close this discussion is by seeking the advice of Warren Buffett, the world's most famous investor. In his 2013 letter to Berkshire shareholders Mr. Buffett said,

> *Most investors, of course, have not made the study of business prospects a priority in their lives. If wise, they will conclude that they do not know enough about specific businesses to predict their future earning power.*
>
> *I have good news for these non-professionals: The typical investor doesn't need this skill. In aggregate, American business has done wonderfully over time and will continue to do so (though, most assuredly, in unpredictable fits and starts). In the 20th Century, the Dow Jones Industrials index advanced from 66 to 11,497, paying a rising stream of dividends to boot. The 21st Century will witness further gains, almost certain to be substantial. The goal of the non-professional should not be to pick winners – neither he nor his "helpers" can do that – but should rather be to own a cross-section of businesses that in aggregate are bound to do well. A low-cost S&P 500 index fund will achieve this goal.*
>
> *That's the "what" of investing for the non-professional. The "when" is also important. The main danger is that the timid or beginning investor will enter the market at a time of extreme exuberance and then become disillusioned when paper losses occur. (Remember the late Barton Biggs' observation: "A bull market is like sex. It feels best just before it ends.") The antidote to that kind of mistiming is for an investor to accumulate shares over a long period and never to sell when the news is bad and stocks are well off their highs. Following those rules, the "know-nothing"*

investor who both diversifies and keeps his costs minimal is virtually certain to get satisfactory results. Indeed, the unsophisticated investor who is realistic about his short-comings is likely to obtain better long-term results than the knowledgeable professional who is blind to even a single weakness.

We do note that Mr. Buffett does not follow his own advice. He is an active investor whose common stock investments are concentrated in a few large holdings. Furthermore, in the spirit of full disclosure, we admit that we are in the Buffett camp. The hedge fund that we run, SMBP, takes active positions. We like to think that is because we share some of Mr. Buffett's insight regarding the fundamental valuation of companies, an issue we discuss in the last chapter, but it may be a case of self-delusion.

ENOUGH OF THE THEORY, WHAT ABOUT RESULTS?

As you might suspect the literature on investment performance, both academic and practitioner, is vast. There is too much money at stake for it not to be. Because the goal of this book is to describe the conceptual foundations of investing, we do not wade very far into this literature. But there is one issue sufficiently important to address. In light of the competitive market hypothesis and the Sharpe arithmetic, how do professional investors actually do? Mutual funds are particularly useful in this context because they have detailed reporting requirements. Exhibit 2.2 from Standard and Poor's gives a good overview of the massive literature on mutual fund performance. The results are broken down by the type of the mutual fund so that they can be compared to an appropriate benchmark. For example, small-cap managers are

EXHIBIT 2.2 Actively managed mutual fund performance relative to their benchmarks.

Number of funds	Fund type	Benchmark	Percentage of funds outperforming the benchmarket				
			1 year	3 years	5 years	10 years	15 years
866	All large-cap	S&P 500	43.44	18.15	17.32	14.92	6.82
543	All small-cap	S&P SmallCap 600	41.45	11.26	6.17	5.94	5.57
243	Large-cap growth	S&P 500 Growth	62.14	25.19	23.57	7.69	4.94
329	Large-cap value	S&P 500 Value	47.71	12.81	11.37	35.75	16.94
187	Small-cap growth	S&P SmallCap 600 Growth	50.17	11.98	9.95	4.52	0.65

From S&P Mid-year scorecard, August 2017.

compared with S&P's small-cap index. Remember that Sharpe's arithmetic applies to segments of the market as well as to the market as a whole. It predicts that passive investors who buy a small-cap index will, on average, outperform active investors who trade small-cap stocks.

The exhibit shows the fraction of actively managed funds that outperformed their passive S&P benchmarks at horizons of 1, 3, 5, 10, and 15 years. The fund categories examined are: all large-cap, all small-cap, large-cap growth, large-cap value, and small-cap growth.[6] At an horizon of 1 year, about 50% of the funds beat their respective benchmarks. That is what you might expect if the world of active traders were divided into winners and losers. But if there were such a division, and if winners maintained their winning ways, then about half of the funds should outperform at longer horizons. That is not the case. As the horizon is lengthened, the fraction of active managers outperforming the benchmark

---

[6]The terms "small-cap" and "large-cap" refer to the market capitalization of the stocks held in the funds. Market capitalization refers to the market value of a firm's equity given as the current price times the shares outstanding. Growth stocks are those with a large market value compared to their current earnings while value stocks are the reverse.

falls consistently. By year 15, with the exception of large-cap value funds, only about 5% of the active managers are beating their benchmarks. Even the large-cap value managers beat their benchmark less than 17% of the time. The apparent reason for the underperformance is the cost of active trading. That cost has to be paid every year, whereas investment performance results go up and down. Eventually those costs, which passive investors can avoid, tend to overwhelm the benefits of active trading. In the case of small-cap growth funds, where the trading costs are highest, less than 1% outperform the benchmark over the 15-year horizon. All of this is consistent with both Sharpe's arithmetic and market efficiency.

Sharpe's arithmetic applies to aggregate groups, not individual managers. It is possible for Sharpe's arithmetic to hold and for some particularly talented managers to consistently outperform. Market efficiency makes a stronger statement. In a relatively efficient market, no active trader should be able to consistently beat the market. Here is a way to test whether that stronger statement is true. In year one, divide active managers into two groups: those that beat the market (the winners) and those that did not (the losers). Based on Exhibit 2.2, about half of the managers will be winners. If the first-year winners are truly more talented, then more than half of them should be winners the second year. Next, consider those managers who were winners the first two years: they should be even more likely to beat the market in year three. Proceed in this fashion out five years. This procedure has been implemented in numerous studies, always with the same basic result. Of the first-year winners, about 50% win in year two. (As do about 50% of the first-year losers.) Of those who won the first two years, about 50% win in year three. Going forward, it is the same year after year. It does not matter whether a manager won or lost last year, the probability of winning the next year is about 50%. This is exactly what should happen if winning and losing was random because the securities were fairly priced. That is what the EMH predicts, and to a surprising extent that is what the data show.

Skeptical readers may say that the foregoing procedure fails to identify truly superior investors. After all, there are Warren Buffetts out there. But care should be taken when considering outliers like Mr. Buffett. Lottery winners have extraordinary investment performance, but that does not mean they are superior investors or that buying lottery tickets is a wise investment strategy. Given a large enough sample of investors, and there are millions in the United States alone, one would expect a few instances of dramatically good results by luck alone. This does not necessarily mean that Mr. Buffett was just lucky. His education, analytical skills, patience, thoroughness, and attention to detail all suggest otherwise, but it is a warning to be suspicious of drawing conclusions based on a few extreme observations drawn from a huge sample.

Even the case of Mr. Buffett shows how difficult it is to continually beat a competitive market, particularly as the amount of money you have to invest grows. Exhibit 2.3, based on Mr. Buffett's 2017 letter to Berkshire shareholders, presents his performance

EXHIBIT 2.3 Berkshire performance relative to the S&P 500.

Geometric average return	Berkshire (%)	S&P 500 (%)	Berkshire outperformance (%)
1964–1974	12.45	1.39	11.07
1975–1984	41.01	11.05	29.96
1985–1994	23.50	11.25	12.25
1995–2004	9.93	6.34	3.59
2005–2016	8.80	7.07	1.73
First three decades	28.01	9.94	18.07
Full period	20.94	9.78	11.16

relative to the S&P 500 (Mr. Buffett's chosen benchmark) on a decade-by-decade basis since 1965. Over the first three decades, the performance of Berkshire stock relative to the S&P 500 is dramatic. The geometric average return for Berkshire is 28.01% versus 9.94% for the S&P 500. Given the power of compound interest the impact of that difference is immense. An investment of $1 in the S&P 500 at the start of 1965 would have grown to $17.17 by the end of 1994. In comparison, the same investment in Berkshire stock would have grown to $1,647.93! But in last two decades, Mr. Buffett's performance has slipped. In the decade ending 2004 his outperformance relative to the S&P 500 was only 3.59% and in the final decade (actually 12 years) it dropped to 1.73%.

Finally, regarding the role of diversification, there is a more subtle point to be made. There is a tendency to think of the market as a tide and that all stocks rise or fall with that tide. This is not the case. Based on a comprehensive study of all the stocks in the CRSP database from 1926 to 2016, Prof. Hendrik Bessembinder finds that

1. Just 42.6% of the stocks have a life-time return that exceeds the return to holding one-month Treasury bills over the same horizon.
2. Of the 25,332 companies that appear in the database, 1092, or slightly more than 4%, account for *all* of the wealth creation.
3. Just 90 companies, or about 0.36% of the total, account for half of the total wealth creation.

What Prof. Bessembinder's work shows is that if you diversify widely you will get the benefit of owning the relatively few stocks that count for the vast majority of the wealth creation. If you are an active investor and specialize in the holding of relatively few securities, and happen to miss the major wealth creators, then your long-run return is likely be below that of one-month Treasury bills. The benefit of holding a relatively limited number of securities is that if you can identify high wealth creators, you will clearly beat the market because the market portfolio is diluted by all the underperformers. But that benefit comes with added risk of significant underperformance.

CONCEPTUAL FOUNDATION 2

The second conceptual foundation of investing is an understanding of the economic structure of financial markets. Investors as a group must always earn the market return. If you passively hold a market index fund, Sharpe's arithmetic implies you are assured of outperforming the average investor, and outperforming the average active investor by even more. If you choose to be an active investor, the arithmetic says you can do better than a passive investor only to the extent that some other active investor does worse. And both of you have to pay the costs of being active. To make matters worse, the counterparty to your trade is likely to be a sophisticated financial institution that obviously disagrees with you. The good news is that the EMH offers some protection. If the market is so competitive that almost all securities are fairly priced, then it is difficult to find mispriced securities, but it is also difficult for a more astute counterparty to sell you a mispriced security.

3

BONDS AND INFLATION

Inflation is generally described as an increase in the prices of goods and services generally, but that is a misleading way of thinking about it. Inflation is more appropriately thought of as a decline in one price – the purchasing power of the unit of account, the dollar.

To see how it works, let's do a thought experiment. In the case of distance measurement, the most widely used unit of account is the meter. Until the twentieth century, the meter was defined to be the length of a platinum bar kept in an air-tight, temperature-controlled vault in Paris. If a dispute arose regarding whether some object was a meter long, in principle the vault could be opened and the bar could be used to confirm whether the object in question was the same length.

Now assume that some alien force is able to start shrinking the platinum bar as part of an effort to confuse humanity. How would we experience the shrinkage? By definition, the bar in the vault would always be a "meter." But when the official meter is used to measure the length of other objects they would all appear to be getting longer. Suppose, for instance, that the bar was shrinking at 2% per year. In that case, every object would be measured as being 2% longer each year. This could get confusing because true lengths could also be changing for other reasons. For example, a growing child would be measured as taller both because the child was growing and because the meter was shrinking.

One way to confront the complexity would be to define what might be called a "constant year meter." For instance, a constant year meter could be defined as the length of the bar on January 1, 2017. Other lengths could then be stated in terms of "2017 meters." That would be a way to get around the shrinkage problem.

Now it may seem to you like this is all a bunch of theoretical nonsense. And from the point of view of the meter, that is probably right. But with respect to the dollar, it is exactly what has been happening almost every year for the past century. As the dollar shrinks, we experience it as increases in the price of goods and services because all of those prices are measured in dollars. In addition, like the growing child, prices change both because the dollar is shrinking and because the prices are moving for other reasons. Therefore, the Bureau of Labor Statistics (BLS), which keeps track of consumer goods and services prices, does, in fact, use a constant year dollar. The BLS speaks of prices defined in terms of both current dollars (today's unit) and constant year dollars (reflecting the purchasing power of the dollar in 2010).

To measure the change in prices generally, the BLS constructs what is known as the Consumer Price Index, or CPI. The CPI measures the cost of purchasing a diverse bundle of goods and services. The index is adjusted to take account of the fact that over time the make-up and quality of the goods and services that people consume changes. The inflation rate is defined to be the percentage change in the consumer price index.

The reason that taking account of inflation is so important to investors is because people consume goods and services, not dollars. Because the dollar is constantly shrinking, you can't measure the success of investment by simply looking at the path of wealth (POW) measure in terms of dollars. The dollars at the end of the period are worth less than the dollars at the beginning. Instead, it is necessary to work with what are called *real*, or inflation-adjusted, returns. A real POW can then be constructed using the real returns. By way of distinction, returns and POWs stated in terms of current dollars are referred to as *nominal*. The easiest way to understand how all this works is by going through an example. But before that, let's get started by looking at some actual data on inflation.

The first column of Exhibit 3.1 presents the annual rate of inflation from 1926 to 2017. The exhibit shows that inflation has been far from constant in the United States. At the beginning of the sample period, inflation was negative (there was deflation) for the first seven years. The rate of deflation reached 10% at the height of the great depression in 1932. With the onset of World War II, inflation turned sharply positive, rising as high as 18.13% in 1946. During the 1950s and early 1960s, inflation was quiescent, averaging less than 2%. Then it turned up again during the escalation of the Vietnam War. From 1973 until 1981, the United States experienced its most prolonged period of significant inflation when the average was close to 10%. In recent years, following the financial crisis, inflation has fallen back to less than 2% per year. Currently, the Federal Reserve has an inflation target of 2% per year. Over the full period from 1926 until 2017, the arithmetic average rate of inflation was 2.97%.

EXHIBIT 3.1 U.S. inflation: 1926–2017.

Date	Inflation (%)	Purchasing power of $1
		1.000
1926	−1.12	1.011
1927	−2.26	1.035
1928	−1.16	1.047
1929	0.58	1.041
1930	−6.40	1.112
1931	−9.32	1.226
1932	−10.27	1.366
1933	0.76	1.356
1934	1.52	1.336
1935	2.99	1.297
1936	1.45	1.279
1937	2.86	1.243
1938	−2.78	1.279
1939	0.00	1.279
1940	0.71	1.270
1941	9.93	1.155
1942	9.03	1.059
1943	2.96	1.029
1944	2.30	1.006
1945	2.25	0.984
1946	18.13	0.833
1947	8.84	0.765
1948	2.99	0.743
1949	−2.07	0.758
1950	5.93	0.716
1951	6.00	0.675
1952	0.75	0.670
1953	0.75	0.665
1954	−0.74	0.670
1955	0.37	0.668
1956	2.98	0.649
1957	2.90	0.630
1958	1.76	0.619
1959	1.73	0.609
1960	1.36	0.601
1961	0.67	0.597
1962	1.33	0.589
1963	1.64	0.579
1964	0.97	0.574
1965	1.92	0.563

EXHIBIT 3.1 (Continued)

Date	Inflation (%)	Purchasing power of $1
1966	3.46	0.544
1967	3.04	0.528
1968	4.72	0.504
1969	6.20	0.475
1970	5.57	0.450
1971	3.27	0.436
1972	3.41	0.421
1973	8.71	0.387
1974	12.34	0.345
1975	6.94	0.323
1976	4.86	0.308
1977	6.70	0.288
1978	9.02	0.264
1979	13.29	0.233
1980	12.52	0.207
1981	8.92	0.190
1982	3.83	0.183
1983	3.79	0.177
1984	3.95	0.170
1985	3.80	0.164
1986	1.10	0.162
1987	4.43	0.155
1988	4.42	0.149
1989	4.65	0.142
1990	6.11	0.134
1991	3.06	0.130
1992	2.90	0.126
1993	2.75	0.123
1994	2.67	0.120
1995	2.54	0.117
1996	3.32	0.113
1997	1.70	0.111
1998	1.61	0.109
1999	2.68	0.106
2000	3.39	0.103
2001	1.55	0.101
2002	2.38	0.099
2003	1.88	0.097
2004	3.26	0.094
2005	3.42	0.091

EXHIBIT 3.1 (Continued)

Date	Inflation (%)	Purchasing power of $1
2006	2.54	0.089
2007	4.08	0.085
2008	0.09	0.085
2009	2.72	0.083
2010	1.50	0.082
2011	2.96	0.079
2012	1.74	0.078
2013	1.50	0.077
2014	0.76	0.076
2015	0.73	0.076
2016	2.11	0.074
2017	2.11	0.073
Average	2.97	

The second column of the exhibit shows the value of a dollar for each current year in terms of 1926 dollars. Notice that by 1933 the purchasing power of a current dollar had risen to $1.356 in terms of 1926 dollars. But with the onset of inflation the dollar began to shrink. By 2017, the purchasing power of a current dollar was worth only 7.3 cents in terms of 1926 dollars.

It is worth noting that although inflation in the United States ranged from about −10% to 10% that variation is small by international and historical standards. Inflation rates of 100% per year or more are not that rare and inflation exceeding 1,000,000% per year have been recorded in recent decades. As we write this, 100 trillion dollar notes in Zimbabwe dollars can be purchased on eBay for about $20 U.S. dollars. In Germany after the First World War, prices rose by a factor of 10^{12}, aiding Hitler's rise to power.

To illustrate how inflation impacts the real returns on investments, the second column of Exhibit 3.2 starts by reproducing

EXHIBIT 3.2 Real returns on the market: 1926–2017.

Date	Market nominal return (%)	Market real return (%)	Nominal market POW	Real market POW
			1.00	1.00
1926	9.85	11.09	1.10	1.11
1927	32.87	35.94	1.46	1.51
1928	39.14	40.77	2.03	2.13
1929	−15.10	−15.59	1.72	1.79
1930	−28.90	−24.04	1.23	1.36
1931	−44.39	−38.67	0.68	0.84
1932	−7.94	2.60	0.63	0.86
1933	57.41	56.22	0.99	1.34
1934	3.18	1.64	1.02	1.36
1935	45.45	41.23	1.48	1.92
1936	32.32	30.43	1.96	2.51
1937	−34.60	−36.42	1.28	1.59
1938	28.44	32.11	1.65	2.11
1939	1.84	1.84	1.68	2.15
1940	−7.51	−8.17	1.55	1.97
1941	−10.04	−18.16	1.40	1.61
1942	16.72	7.05	1.63	1.73
1943	27.97	24.29	2.09	2.15
1944	21.36	18.64	2.53	2.55
1945	39.06	36.00	3.52	3.46
1946	−6.42	−20.78	3.29	2.74
1947	3.29	−5.09	3.40	2.60
1948	2.13	−0.84	3.47	2.58
1949	20.11	22.65	4.17	3.17
1950	30.47	23.17	5.45	3.90
1951	20.94	14.10	6.59	4.45
1952	13.33	12.48	7.46	5.00
1953	0.38	−0.36	7.49	4.99
1954	50.41	51.54	11.27	7.56
1955	25.41	24.95	14.13	9.44
1956	8.58	5.43	15.35	9.95
1957	−10.35	−12.87	13.76	8.67
1958	44.78	42.27	19.92	12.34
1959	12.65	10.73	22.44	13.66
1960	1.21	−0.15	22.71	13.64
1961	26.96	26.11	28.83	17.20
1962	−9.93	−11.11	25.97	15.29
1963	21.40	19.43	31.53	18.26

EXHIBIT 3.2 (Continued)

Date	Market nominal return (%)	Market real return (%)	Nominal market POW	Real market POW
1964	16.35	15.23	36.68	21.04
1965	14.06	11.91	41.84	23.55
1966	−8.86	−11.90	38.13	20.75
1967	26.84	23.10	48.36	25.54
1968	12.75	7.67	54.53	27.50
1969	−9.82	−15.08	49.18	23.35
1970	1.29	−4.06	49.81	22.40
1971	15.84	12.18	57.70	25.13
1972	17.64	13.76	67.88	28.59
1973	−16.92	−23.57	56.39	21.85
1974	−26.81	−34.85	41.27	14.24
1975	37.66	28.73	56.82	18.33
1976	26.25	20.39	71.73	22.06
1977	−4.84	−10.82	68.26	19.68
1978	7.33	−1.55	73.27	19.37
1979	21.88	7.58	89.30	20.84
1980	32.63	17.88	118.44	24.57
1981	−4.14	−12.00	113.53	21.62
1982	21.00	16.54	137.37	25.19
1983	22.76	18.27	168.63	29.80
1984	5.79	1.77	178.39	30.32
1985	31.74	26.92	235.01	38.49
1986	17.32	16.05	275.72	44.66
1987	2.89	−1.48	283.69	44.00
1988	17.57	12.59	333.53	49.55
1989	29.61	23.86	432.29	61.36
1990	−4.27	−9.78	413.85	55.37
1991	30.65	26.77	540.71	70.19
1992	8.22	5.17	585.14	73.81
1993	10.75	7.79	648.04	79.56
1994	−0.09	−2.69	647.47	77.42
1995	35.07	31.72	874.51	101.98
1996	21.35	17.44	1061.19	119.77
1997	32.32	30.10	1404.13	155.82
1998	19.13	17.25	1672.80	182.69
1999	10.38	7.49	1846.43	196.38
2000	3.47	0.09	1910.59	196.55
2001	−8.45	−9.85	1749.15	177.19
2002	−18.22	−20.11	1430.54	141.55
2003	29.13	26.75	1847.32	179.42

EXHIBIT 3.2 (Continued)

Date	Market nominal return (%)	Market real return (%)	Nominal market POW	Real market POW
2004	13.88	10.29	2103.67	197.87
2005	8.45	4.87	2281.49	207.51
2006	17.62	14.71	2683.55	238.03
2007	6.62	2.44	2861.21	243.84
2008	−37.83	−37.88	1778.89	151.46
2009	28.13	24.73	2279.23	188.92
2010	17.78	16.04	2684.42	219.23
2011	−0.89	−3.74	2660.65	211.04
2012	15.51	13.54	3073.41	239.61
2013	29.45	27.54	3978.64	305.59
2014	9.45	8.63	4354.70	331.96
2015	−4.55	−5.24	4156.62	314.57
2016	14.48	12.15	4758.33	352.79
2017	17.67	12.15	5599.04	395.65
Average	11.69	8.56		

the nominal returns on the Center for Research in Securities Prices (CRSP) market index from the chapter on returns. Given the nominal returns, the formula for computing the real return is

$$\text{Real return} = (1 + \text{Nominal Return})/(1 + \text{Inflation}) - 1. \quad (3.1)$$

Applying this formula leads to the series of real returns on the market shown in column three. Finally, the POW is computed using both the nominal returns in column four and the real returns in column five. The results show that the impact of inflation is significant. In nominal terms $1 invested in 1926 rises to $5,599.04. But in terms of 1926 dollars, the 2017 value of the investment is only $395.65. That lower figure represents the actual increase in consumable wealth.

Exhibit 3.3 plots the POW for the CRSP market index in both nominal and real terms. Notice that it is when the periods of high inflation begin that the lines diverge most noticeably. The long-run impact of the compounding of inflation comes through clearly.

EXHIBIT 3.3 Nominal and real POWs for the CRSP index: 1926–2017.

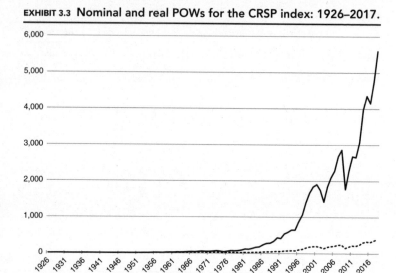

By tradition, most investment performance results are stated in terms of nominal returns. This can cause a good deal of mischief. High returns in a high-inflation environment may well provide less increase in consumable wealth than low returns with low inflation. As we shall see later, inflation also interacts with taxes because most taxes are levied in nominal terms. This also impacts consumable wealth. The bottom line is that inflation is not something investors can ignore, even when it is as low as 2%.

The relation between security returns and inflation is particularly important in the case of fixed income securities. Inflation impacts fixed income securities in two ways. First, the rate of inflation expected over the life of a fixed income security is a prime determinant of the rate of interest paid by the security. Second, the real purchasing power of the dollars received from the security depends on the subsequent rate of inflation that occurs over the life of the security. To explain this further, it is first necessary to know more about how fixed income securities work. There is no better place to start than with the most important fixed income securities in the world – U.S. Treasury bonds and U.S. Treasury bills.

TREASURY BILLS AND TREASURY BONDS

Because the United States has run large deficits for decades there are now over $20 trillion dollars of Treasury securities outstanding. Ironically, the debt is almost exactly equal to the total value of stocks traded on the New York Stock Exchange. These securities are generally referred to as risk free because the U.S. government stands behind them and could, if necessary, print money to redeem them. But with the exception of Treasury Inflation Protected Securities, or TIPS, they are risk free only in nominal terms. There is no certainty regarding the purchasing power of the dollars that investors will receive.

Exhibit 3.4 shows that there are two types of Treasury securities: Treasury bills and Treasury notes and bonds. Treasury bills have a maturity of one year or less, while Treasury notes range in maturity from 2 to 10 years and Treasury bonds have maturities from 10 to 30 years.

The data reported in the exhibit are based on prices quoted in the secondary market. After their initial auction, Treasury securities are actively traded through a network of government securities dealers. Each of these dealers quotes prices at which the firm is willing to buy or sell outstanding Treasury issues. The dollar volume of trading in Treasury securities outstrips the volume of trading on the New York Stock Exchange despite the fact that there are a relatively limited number of issues. This makes the market one of the most liquid in the world.

EXHIBIT 3.4 Treasury bonds and notes and Treasury bills as of November 20, 2017.

Treasury Notes and Bonds				
Maturity	Coupon	Bid	Asked	Asked Yield
11/30/2017	0.875	99.977	99.992	1.191
11/30/2017	2.250	100.008	100.023	1.287
12/15/2017	1.000	99.992	100.008	0.879
12/31/2017	0.750	99.938	99.953	1.181
12/31/2017	1.000	99.969	99.984	1.142
12/31/2017	2.750	100.164	100.180	1.086
1/15/2018	0.875	99.953	99.969	1.083
1/31/2018	0.750	99.906	99.922	1.155
1/31/2018	0.875	99.930	99.945	1.158
1/31/2018	2.625	100.258	100.273	1.197
2/15/2018	1.000	99.930	99.945	1.233
2/15/2018	3.500	100.508	100.523	1.244
2/28/2018	0.750	99.836	99.852	1.294
2/28/2018	2.750	100.375	100.391	1.310
3/15/2018	1.000	99.898	99.914	1.273
3/31/2018	0.750	99.766	99.781	1.365
3/31/2018	0.875	99.813	99.828	1.358
3/31/2018	2.875	100.523	100.539	1.354
4/15/2018	0.750	99.766	99.781	1.302
4/30/2018	0.625	99.664	99.680	1.354
4/30/2018	0.750	99.711	99.727	1.372
4/30/2018	2.625	100.523	100.539	1.396
5/15/2018	1.000	99.805	99.820	1.374
5/15/2018	3.875	101.195	101.211	1.353
5/15/2018	9.125	103.656	103.672	1.473
5/31/2018	0.875	99.719	99.734	1.385
5/31/2018	1.000	99.781	99.797	1.390
5/31/2018	2.375	100.477	100.492	1.430
6/15/2018	1.125	99.805	99.820	1.445
6/30/2018	0.625	99.477	99.492	1.466
6/30/2018	1.375	99.938	99.953	1.452
6/30/2018	2.375	100.523	100.539	1.481
7/15/2018	0.875	99.602	99.617	1.469
7/31/2018	0.750	99.477	99.492	1.489
7/31/2018	1.375	99.906	99.922	1.488
7/31/2018	2.250	100.516	100.531	1.475
8/15/2018	1.000	99.602	99.617	1.526
8/15/2018	4.000	101.766	101.781	1.546

EXHIBIT 3.4 (Continued)

Maturity	Coupon	Bid	Asked	Asked Yield
		Treasury Notes and Bonds		
8/31/2018	0.750	99.367	99.383	1.555
8/31/2018	1.500	99.930	99.945	1.571
9/15/2018	1.000	99.508	99.523	1.590
9/30/2018	0.750	99.273	99.289	1.588
9/30/2018	1.375	99.789	99.805	1.605
10/15/2018	0.875	99.344	99.359	1.596
10/31/2018	0.750	99.188	99.203	1.606
10/31/2018	1.250	99.625	99.641	1.636
10/31/2018	1.750	100.117	100.133	1.607
11/15/2018	1.250	99.617	99.633	1.628
11/15/2018	3.750	102.039	102.055	1.635
11/15/2018	9.000	107.219	107.234	1.558
11/30/2018	1.000	99.344	99.359	1.633
11/30/2018	1.250	99.602	99.617	1.628
11/30/2018	1.375	99.742	99.758	1.614
12/15/2018	1.250	99.586	99.602	1.628
12/31/2018	1.250	99.555	99.570	1.642
12/31/2018	1.375	99.672	99.688	1.660
12/31/2018	1.500	99.828	99.844	1.642
1/15/2019	1.125	99.391	99.406	1.648
1/31/2019	1.125	99.352	99.367	1.663
1/31/2019	1.250	99.508	99.523	1.655
1/31/2019	1.500	99.789	99.805	1.665
2/15/2019	0.750	98.867	98.883	1.668
2/15/2019	2.750	101.305	101.32	1.663
2/15/2019	8.875	108.867	108.883	1.573
2/28/2019	1.125	99.297	99.313	1.672
2/28/2019	1.375	99.602	99.617	1.680
2/28/2019	1.500	99.766	99.781	1.674
3/15/2019	1.000	99.094	99.109	1.687
3/31/2019	1.250	99.406	99.422	1.682
3/31/2019	1.500	99.734	99.750	1.687
3/31/2019	1.625	99.906	99.922	1.683
4/15/2019	0.875	98.867	98.883	1.687
4/30/2019	1.250	99.344	99.359	1.701
4/30/2019	1.625	99.898	99.914	1.685
5/15/2019	0.875	98.805	98.820	1.684
5/15/2019	3.125	102.102	102.117	1.674

EXHIBIT 3.4 (Continued)

		Treasury Notes and Bonds		
Maturity	Coupon	Bid	Asked	Asked Yield
5/31/2019	1.125	99.148	99.164	1.683
5/31/2019	1.250	99.320	99.336	1.693
5/31/2019	1.500	99.695	99.711	1.693
6/15/2019	0.875	98.711	98.727	1.706
6/30/2019	1.000	98.867	98.883	1.707
6/30/2019	1.250	99.273	99.289	1.700
6/30/2019	1.625	99.852	99.867	1.709
7/15/2019	0.750	98.422	98.438	1.715
7/31/2019	0.875	98.602	98.617	1.707
7/31/2019	1.375	99.422	99.438	1.713
7/31/2019	1.625	99.805	99.820	1.733
8/15/2019	0.750	98.344	98.359	1.714
8/15/2019	3.625	103.234	103.250	1.713
8/15/2019	8.125	110.922	110.938	1.694
8/31/2019	1.000	98.734	98.750	1.718
8/31/2019	1.250	99.156	99.172	1.726
8/31/2019	1.625	99.789	99.805	1.737
9/15/2019	0.875	98.430	98.445	1.749
9/30/2019	1.000	98.641	98.656	1.738
9/30/2019	1.375	99.313	99.328	1.744
9/30/2019	1.750	99.984	100.000	1.750
10/15/2019	1.000	98.586	98.602	1.752
10/31/2019	1.250	99.047	99.063	1.743
10/31/2019	1.500	99.500	99.516	1.755
11/15/2019	1.000	98.523	98.539	1.753
11/15/2019	3.375	103.125	103.141	1.757
11/30/2019	1.000	98.477	98.492	1.761
11/30/2019	1.500	99.461	99.477	1.764
12/15/2019	1.375	99.195	99.211	1.766
12/31/2019	1.125	98.672	98.688	1.762
12/31/2019	1.625	99.656	99.672	1.784
1/15/2020	1.375	99.141	99.156	1.777
1/31/2020	1.250	98.836	98.852	1.786
1/31/2020	1.375	99.125	99.141	1.776
2/15/2020	1.375	99.094	99.109	1.783
2/15/2020	3.625	104.031	104.047	1.768
2/15/2020	8.500	114.844	114.859	1.691
2/29/2020	1.250	98.797	98.813	1.785
2/29/2020	1.375	99.086	99.102	1.780
3/15/2020	1.625	99.609	99.625	1.791
3/31/2020	1.125	98.469	98.484	1.784

EXHIBIT 3.4 (Continued)

		Treasury Notes and Bonds		
Maturity	Coupon	Bid	Asked	Asked Yield
3/31/2020	1.375	99.008	99.023	1.800
4/30/2020	1.125	98.391	98.406	1.795
4/30/2020	1.375	98.977	98.992	1.799
5/15/2020	1.500	99.258	99.273	1.800
5/15/2020	3.500	104.102	104.117	1.797
5/15/2020	8.750	116.992	117.008	1.724
6/15/2020	1.500	99.211	99.227	1.810
6/30/2020	1.625	99.492	99.508	1.819
6/30/2020	1.875	100.148	100.164	1.810
7/15/2020	1.500	99.156	99.172	1.821
7/31/2020	1.625	99.453	99.469	1.828
7/31/2020	2.000	100.438	100.453	1.826
8/15/2020	1.500	99.117	99.133	1.826
8/15/2020	2.625	102.102	102.117	1.827
8/15/2020	8.750	118.484	118.500	1.784
8/31/2020	1.375	98.750	98.766	1.833
8/31/2020	2.125	100.766	100.781	1.834
9/15/2020	1.375	98.773	98.789	1.818
9/30/2020	1.375	98.688	98.703	1.843
9/30/2020	2.000	100.430	100.445	1.839
10/15/2020	1.625	99.344	99.359	1.853
10/31/2020	1.375	98.617	98.633	1.855
10/31/2020	1.750	99.695	99.711	1.851
11/15/2020	1.750	99.672	99.688	1.858
11/15/2020	2.625	102.203	102.219	1.857
11/30/2020	1.625	99.273	99.289	1.868
11/30/2020	2.000	100.383	100.398	1.864
12/31/2020	1.750	99.586	99.602	1.882
12/31/2020	2.375	101.484	101.500	1.876
1/31/2021	1.375	98.359	98.375	1.90
1/31/2021	2.125	100.695	100.711	1.89
2/15/2021	3.625	105.422	105.438	1.88
2/15/2021	7.875	118.820	118.836	1.85
2/28/2021	1.125	97.500	97.516	1.91
2/28/2021	2.000	100.289	100.305	1.90
3/31/2021	1.250	97.797	97.813	1.93
3/31/2021	2.250	101.055	101.070	1.92
4/30/2021	1.375	98.117	98.133	1.94
4/30/2021	2.250	101.039	101.055	1.93
5/15/2021	3.125	104.016	104.031	1.92
5/15/2021	8.125	120.945	120.961	1.88

EXHIBIT 3.4 (Continued)

		Treasury Notes and Bonds		
Maturity	Coupon	Bid	Asked	Asked Yield
5/31/2021	1.375	98.039	98.055	1.95
5/31/2021	2.000	100.188	100.203	1.94
6/30/2021	1.125	97.125	97.141	1.95
6/30/2021	2.125	100.570	100.586	1.96
7/31/2021	1.125	96.992	97.008	1.97
7/31/2021	2.250	101.000	101.016	1.96
8/15/2021	2.125	100.531	100.547	1.97
8/15/2021	8.125	122.211	122.227	1.93
8/31/2021	1.125	96.891	96.906	1.98
8/31/2021	2.000	100.070	100.086	1.98
9/30/2021	1.125	96.773	96.789	1.99
9/30/2021	2.125	100.484	100.500	1.99
10/31/2021	1.250	97.164	97.180	2.00
10/31/2021	2.000	100.016	100.031	1.99
11/15/2021	2.000	100.055	100.070	1.98
11/15/2021	8.000	123.063	123.078	1.95
11/30/2021	1.750	98.969	98.984	2.01
11/30/2021	1.875	99.563	99.578	1.99
12/31/2021	2.000	99.891	99.906	2.02
12/31/2021	2.125	100.422	100.438	2.01
1/31/2022	1.500	97.906	97.922	2.02
1/31/2022	1.875	99.352	99.367	2.03
2/15/2022	2.000	99.977	99.992	2.00
2/28/2022	1.750	98.891	98.906	2.02
2/28/2022	1.875	99.320	99.336	2.04
3/31/2022	1.750	98.797	98.813	2.04
3/31/2022	1.875	99.250	99.266	2.05
4/30/2022	1.750	98.703	98.719	2.05
4/30/2022	1.875	99.203	99.219	2.06
5/15/2022	1.750	98.758	98.773	2.04
5/31/2022	1.750	98.664	98.680	2.06
5/31/2022	1.875	99.242	99.258	2.05
6/30/2022	1.750	98.586	98.602	2.07
6/30/2022	2.125	100.234	100.250	2.07
7/31/2022	1.875	99.055	99.070	2.08
7/31/2022	2.000	99.648	99.664	2.08
8/15/2022	1.625	98.031	98.047	2.06
			123.359	2.05
			97.945	2.08
8/31/2022	1.875	99.039	99.055	2.08
9/30/2022	1.750	98.398	98.414	2.10

EXHIBIT 3.4 (Continued)

		Treasury Notes and Bonds		
Maturity	Coupon	Bid	Asked	Asked Yield
9/30/2022	1.875	98.984	99.000	2.09
10/31/2022	1.875	98.938	98.953	2.10
10/31/2022	2.000	99.578	99.594	2.09
11/15/2022	1.625	97.758	97.773	2.10
11/15/2022	7.625	126.109	126.125	2.08
11/30/2022	2.000	99.500	99.516	2.10
12/31/2022	2.125	100.008	100.023	2.12
1/31/2023	1.750	98.109	98.125	2.13
2/15/2023	2.000	99.313	99.328	2.14
2/15/2023	7.125	124.727	124.742	2.11
2/28/2023	1.500	96.805	96.820	2.14
3/31/2023	1.500	96.719	96.734	2.15
4/30/2023	1.625	97.289	97.305	2.15
5/15/2023	1.750	97.930	97.945	2.15
5/31/2023	1.625	97.227	97.242	2.16
6/30/2023	1.375	95.844	95.859	2.16
7/31/2023	1.250	95.063	95.078	2.17
8/15/2023	2.500	101.773	101.789	2.17
8/15/2023	6.250	122.039	122.055	2.14
8/31/2023	1.375	95.656	95.672	2.18
9/30/2023	1.375	95.555	95.570	2.19
10/31/2023	1.625	96.891	96.906	2.183
11/15/2023	2.750	103.164	103.180	2.180
11/30/2023	2.125	99.672	99.688	2.181
12/31/2023	2.250	100.273	100.289	2.199
2/15/2024	2.750	103.086	103.102	2.214
2/29/2024	2.125	99.445	99.461	2.217
3/31/2024	2.125	99.359	99.375	2.231
4/30/2024	2.000	98.594	98.609	2.233
5/15/2024	2.500	101.578	101.594	2.235
5/31/2024	2.000	98.531	98.547	2.241
6/30/2024	2.000	98.484	98.500	2.245
7/31/2024	2.125	99.234	99.250	2.246
8/15/2024	2.375	100.766	100.781	2.249
8/31/2024	1.875	97.641	97.656	2.250
9/30/2024	2.125	99.125	99.141	2.261
10/31/2024	2.250	99.906	99.922	2.262
11/15/2024	2.250	99.883	99.898	2.266
11/15/2024	7.500	134.039	134.055	2.211
2/15/2025	2.000	98.094	98.109	2.285
2/15/2025	7.625	135.891	135.906	2.223

EXHIBIT 3.4 (Continued)

		Treasury Notes and Bonds		
Maturity	Coupon	Bid	Asked	Asked Yield
5/15/2025	2.125	98.813	98.828	2.296
8/15/2025	2.000	97.813	97.828	2.308
8/15/2025	6.875	132.742	132.758	2.238
11/15/2025	2.250	99.461	99.477	2.322
2/15/2026	1.625	94.664	94.680	2.339
2/15/2026	6.000	127.773	127.789	2.279
5/15/2026	1.625	94.422	94.438	2.352
8/15/2026	1.500	93.227	93.242	2.361
8/15/2026	6.750	135.133	135.148	2.287
11/15/2026	2.000	97.000	97.016	2.371
11/15/2026	6.500	133.844	133.859	2.306
2/15/2027	2.250	98.914	98.930	2.380
2/15/2027	6.625	135.734	135.750	2.304
5/15/2027	2.375	99.914	99.930	2.383
8/15/2027	2.250	98.781	98.797	2.389
8/15/2027	6.375	135.039	135.055	2.329
11/15/2027	2.250	98.938	98.953	2.368
11/15/2027	6.125	133.453	133.516	2.341
8/15/2028	5.500	129.391	129.453	2.375
11/15/2028	5.250	127.414	127.477	2.391
2/15/2029	5.250	127.898	127.961	2.396
8/15/2029	6.125	137.867	137.930	2.397
5/15/2030	6.250	141.188	141.250	2.405
2/15/2031	5.375	133.266	133.328	2.417
2/15/2036	4.500	128.859	128.922	2.513
2/15/2037	4.750	133.133	133.195	2.555
5/15/2037	5.000	137.047	137.109	2.567
2/15/2038	4.375	127.578	127.641	2.608
5/15/2038	4.500	129.703	129.766	2.614
2/15/2039	3.500	113.656	113.719	2.651
5/15/2039	4.250	125.922	125.984	2.655
8/15/2039	4.500	130.125	130.188	2.662
11/15/2039	4.375	128.117	128.180	2.672
2/15/2040	4.625	132.422	132.484	2.677
5/15/2040	4.375	128.313	128.375	2.686
8/15/2040	3.875	119.828	119.891	2.699
11/15/2040	4.250	126.391	126.453	2.698
2/15/2041	4.750	135.203	135.234	2.699
5/15/2041	4.375	128.828	128.859	2.706
8/15/2041	3.750	117.906	117.938	2.719
11/15/2041	3.125	106.828	106.859	2.733

EXHIBIT 3.4 (Continued)

	Treasury Notes and Bonds			
Maturity	Coupon	Bid	Asked	Asked Yield
2/15/2042	3.125	106.750	106.781	2.740
5/15/2042	3.000	104.523	104.555	2.743
8/15/2042	2.750	99.859	99.891	2.756
11/15/2042	2.750	99.805	99.836	2.759
2/15/2043	3.125	106.594	106.625	2.759
5/15/2043	2.875	101.930	101.961	2.767
8/15/2043	3.625	115.883	115.914	2.757
11/15/2043	3.750	118.359	118.391	2.754
2/15/2044	3.625	116.094	116.125	2.757
5/15/2044	3.375	111.414	111.445	2.763
8/15/2044	3.125	106.664	106.695	2.769
11/15/2044	3.000	104.250	104.281	2.774
2/15/2045	2.500	94.484	94.516	2.789
5/15/2045	3.000	104.195	104.227	2.779
8/15/2045	2.875	101.727	101.758	2.784
11/15/2045	3.000	104.188	104.219	2.782
2/15/2046	2.500	94.250	94.281	2.794
5/15/2046	2.500	94.180	94.211	2.796
8/15/2046	2.250	89.227	89.258	2.796
11/15/2046	2.875	101.641	101.672	2.791
2/15/2047	3.000	104.180	104.211	2.788
5/15/2047	3.000	104.180	104.211	2.790
8/15/2047	2.750	99.156	99.188	2.790
11/15/2047	2.750	99.195	99.227	2.788

	Treasury Bills			
Maturity	Bid	Ask	Chg	Asked Yield
11/24/2017	1.063	1.053	0.028	1.067
11/30/2017	1.065	1.055	0.027	1.07
12/7/2017	1.045	1.035	−0.013	1.05
12/14/2017	1.043	1.033	−0.008	1.048
12/21/2017	1.088	1.078	−0.015	1.093
12/28/2017	1.165	1.155	0.02	1.172
1/4/2018	1.16	1.15	0.017	1.168
1/11/2018	1.16	1.15	−0.01	1.168
1/18/2018	1.18	1.17	0.013	1.189
1/25/2018	1.198	1.188	0.018	1.207
2/1/2018	1.22	1.21	−0.002	1.23
2/8/2018	1.225	1.215	−0.007	1.235
2/15/2018	1.255	1.245	−0.005	1.266

EXHIBIT 3.4 (Continued)

		Treasury Bills		
Maturity	Bid	Ask	Chg	Asked Yield
2/22/2018	1.255	1.245	0.01	1.266
3/1/2018	1.28	1.27	−0.002	1.292
3/8/2018	1.303	1.293	−0.002	1.316
3/15/2018	1.295	1.285	−0.003	1.308
3/22/2018	1.29	1.28	−0.01	1.303
3/29/2018	1.295	1.285	0.01	1.309
4/5/2018	1.303	1.293	0.013	1.317
4/12/2018	1.313	1.303	−0.002	1.327
4/19/2018	1.3	1.29	−0.013	1.315
4/26/2018	1.315	1.305	unch.	1.331
5/3/2018	1.348	1.338	0.005	1.364
5/10/2018	1.39	1.38	0.013	1.408
5/17/2018	1.403	1.393	0.015	1.422
5/24/2018	1.418	1.408	0.023	1.437
6/21/2018	1.375	1.365	−0.002	1.395
7/19/2018	1.455	1.445	unch.	1.479
8/16/2018	1.485	1.475	0.013	1.512
9/13/2018	1.513	1.503	0.015	1.542
10/11/2018	1.553	1.543	0.013	1.586
11/8/2018	1.563	1.553	0.005	1.598

Treasury bill bid and ask data are representative over-the-counter quotations as of 3pm Eastern time quoted as a discount to face value. Treasury bill yields are to maturity and based on the asked quote.

Treasury note and bond data are representative over-the-counter quotations as of 3pm Eastern time. For notes and bonds callable prior to maturity, yields are computed to the earliest call date for issues quoted above par and to the maturity date for issues below par.

Source: http://www.wsj.com/mdc/public/page/2_3020-treasury-20171120 .html?mod=mdc_pastcalendar

Treasury Bills

Treasury bills are discount securities, which means they are issued at a price less than par and appreciate to par at maturity. For example, a 91-day Treasury bill with a par value of $10,000 discounted at 2.00% will be issued at a price of $9,949.44. Between the issuance date and maturity no other payments are made to the holders of the bills. The Treasury issues bills with three different maturities: three months, six months, and one year. New three- and six-month bills are offered each week; one-year bills are offered once a month. Because the secondary market is highly liquid, bills with any maturity up to one year can easily be purchased with minimal transaction costs.

The bid and ask quotes for Treasury bills, such as those shown in the far-right-hand column of Exhibit 3.4, are stated in terms of the "bank discount" which is quoted on a 360-day basis. The bid price is the price at which a government security dealer is willing to purchase the security and the ask price is the price at which a government security dealer will sell the security. The bid and ask quotes reported in the *Wall Street Journal* are indicative. Actual bid-ask spreads on round lot trades of $10 million or more, which are obtained by contacting government securities dealers, typically are narrower.

The bank discount and the price of the bill per hundred dollars of par value are related by the formula:

$$p = 100 - d \cdot (n/360) \qquad (3.2)$$

where,

p = the price of the Treasury bill per $100 par value,
d = the bank discount, and
n = the number of days until the bill matures.

For example, consider the bill maturing February 15, 2018. As of November 20, 2017, that bill had a maturity of 87 days and was selling at an ask bank discount of 1.245. Substituting these numbers into Eq. (3.2) gives:

$$p = 100 - 1.245 \cdot (87/360) = 99.699$$

Though it looks like an interest rate when reported in the newspaper, the bank discount is not a yield; it is simply a convention used by government securities dealers to quote prices. For this reason, bond equivalent yields on Treasury bills are also reported. These bond equivalent yields, which are shown in the last column of Exhibit 3.4, are comparable to the yield to maturity (YTM) on bonds. The bond equivalent yield for a bill with a maturity of 182 days or less is calculated using the formula:

$$\text{Bond equivalent yield} = \{(100 - p)/p\} \cdot 365/n, \qquad (3.3)$$

where the variables are as defined above. Bond equivalent yields are calculated from the perspective of a buyer of securities and, therefore, are based on ask prices. Utilizing the data above for the 87-day bill, the bond equivalent yield comes to 1.266% as shown in Exhibit 3.4.

Neither the bank discount nor the bond equivalent yield measures the true annual return on a Treasury bill. The true annual return is that rate which an investor would earn over the course of a year if he or she invested in Treasury bills of a given type and reinvested the proceeds in identical bills until the end of the year. Because of the assumed reinvestment, the true annualized yield takes account of compound interest.

The true annualized yield on a Treasury bill can be computed by a two-step procedure. First, Eq. (3.2) is solved for the price of the bill. Second, the true annualized yield is calculated from the price (per hundred), p, the par value, 100, and the maturity in days, n, using the familiar compounding formula:

$$\text{True annualized yield} = \{(100/p)(365/n)\} - 1. \qquad (3.4)$$

Applying Eq. (3.4) to the 85-day bill with a price of 99.119 discussed above, the true annualized yield is 1.27%. Notice that the true annualized yield is at most 2.5 basis points greater than the bank discount and less than 1 basis point greater than the bond equivalent yield. Though these differences are small, they can grow rapidly as rates rise. For example, at a bank discount on the order of 12.00 for 90-day bills, as existed during the late 1970s, the discrepancy between the discount and the true annualized yield is over 50 basis points. When the Treasury bill rate is used as the "risk-free" rate in an economic model, the appropriate measure of return is the true annualized yield because it takes proper account of the compounding of interest.

Treasury Notes and Bonds

Unlike Treasury bills, Treasury notes and bonds pay interest in the form of semi-annual coupons. The bonds come in units with a par value of $1000, but the prices are quoted per hundred. For example, consider the last Treasury bond listed in Exhibit 3.4, the 2.75% coupon maturing in November 2047. As of November 20, 2017, the date on which the data were collected by the *Wall Street Journal*, this was the most recently issued 30-year Treasury bond. The most recently issued 30-year bond is often called the "long" bond or the "bellwether" bond and is closely followed as a benchmark of the market for long-term funds. As shown in the table, the long bond is quoted at prices of 99.195 bid (per hundred) and 99.227 ask.

The semi-annual interest payments on a Treasury bond are determined by the coupon rate. Each interest payment equals the coupon rate times the par value of the bond divided by two. In the case of the long bond, the coupon is 2.75%, which means that the bond pays $13.75 in interest per $1000 in par value every six months for the next 30 years.

The final number shown in the right-hand column is the yield to maturity (YTM). The YTM is defined as twice the internal rate of return, calculated at the ask price. The factor of two is included to adjust for the fact the payments are received semi-annually. As will become apparent, however, this adjustment does not take account of compound interest.

The internal rate of return (IRR) on an investment is that rate which discounts the cash flows from the investment back to the purchase price.[1] It can be quickly computed using spreadsheet software such as Excel. For instance, the internal rate of return on a $100 investment which provides three annual payments of $40, $50 and $60 is the discount rate r, which solves the equation,

$$100 = \frac{40}{(1+r)} + \frac{50}{(1+r)^2} + \frac{60}{(1+r)^3} \qquad (3.5)$$

Application of the IRR function in Excel reveals that r equals 21.6%.

In the case of Treasury bonds, the IRR is that rate which discounts the promised stream of interest and principal payments back to the price of the bond. Returning, for instance, to the long bond and assuming that its maturity is exactly 30 years, the bond provides 60 interest payments of $13.75 and a final principal payment of $1,000 at maturity. The current ask price of the bond is 99.226 per hundred or $992.26 per bond. Thus the IRR is that rate which discounts a stream involving 59 payments of $13.75 and then one payment of $1,013.75 back to a present value of $99.26. Using Excel that rate is found to be 1.394%. Because the cash flows are semi-annual, the resulting internal rate of return is a semi-annual rate. This semi-annual rate is multiplied by two and rounded to two decimal places to calculate what is called the YTM

---

[1] The internal rate of return is discussed in detail in all the major investment texts.

on the bond, which is 2.788% in the example. Bond traders usually quote bond "prices" in terms of YTM. This is because the number is more useful for investors who are concerned with the rate they will earn if they buy the bond, not the price of the bond per hundred dollars of par value.

As noted above, the calculation of the YTM ignores compound interest. To calculate the true annualized yield on a bond, account must be taken of compounding.

The internal rate of return of 1.394% is a true yield, but it is stated per six months, not per year. Using the compounding formula, the annualized yield is given by

$$\text{annual rate} = (1 + \text{semi-annual IRR})^2 - 1.$$

Applying the formula to a semi-annual rate of 1.394% gives a true annualized rate of 2.808%, which is 2 basis points greater than the YTM.

All the foregoing comments and calculations apply to high-grade corporate bonds as well as Treasury bonds. For now, high grade means that the probability of default is so small it can be ignored. Like Treasuries, high-grade corporate bonds typically pay coupons semi-annually and their YTM is calculated in the same way.

INTEREST RATES AND INFLATION

In our discussion of the relation between interest rates and inflation, we focus on Treasuries and other high-grade bonds. Because there is no risk of default, the prices of these securities are not affected by credit risk, which adds another layer of complexity. We turn to the impact of credit risk later in the chapter.

Because the payouts are fixed at the time they are issued, the real rate of return an investor earns on a bond or bill will depend upon the rate of inflation between the time an investor buys the security and the time it is redeemed. To illustrate, consider the case of a one-year Treasury bill issued at a discount of 2.000%. Using Equations (3.1) and (3.3) above, the annualized interest rate on this security is 2.070%. If the subsequently realized inflation rate is 1.75%, then from Eq. (3.1) the realized real return is 0.314%.

Because it is the real return that determines their consumable wealth, investors will take account of the inflation they expect at the time they purchase the Treasury bill. If inflation was expected to be 10%, it would make little sense to buy a bill yielding 2.5%. For this reason, interest rates on fixed income securities reflect expected inflation. Unfortunately, expected inflation, like expected returns, cannot be measured directly, but it is presumably related to recent past inflation. Therefore, in high-inflation environments there should be high interest rates and in low-inflation environments there should be low interest rates. This turns out to be the case.

Exhibit 3.5 provides an illustration. The bars show the rate of inflation for the year in question, the black line plots the interest on short-term Treasury bills over the years from 1960 to 2017. Notice how the interest rate tends to follow the rate of inflation. When inflation rises, inflationary expectations follow and so do interest rates. Although inflation is not the only thing that affects interest rates, academic studies indicate it is the most important. Exhibit 3.5 is consistent with that finding. Interest rates are high when inflation is high and low when inflation is low.

The relation between interest rates and expected inflation is given by an analog to Eq. (3.1). The relation states that

Nominal interest rate

$$= (1 + \text{Real interest rate}) * (1 + \text{Expected Inflation}) - 1.$$

EXHIBIT 3.5 Inflation and Treasury bill interest rates: 1960–2017.

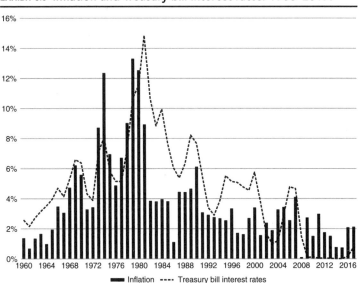

For interest rates and inflation rates less than 10%, such as those experienced in the United States, the equation can be approximated by

Nominal interest rate = Real interest rate + Expected inflation.

$$(3.6)$$

Equation (3.6) provides insight into why most of the variation in nominal interest rates (the financial media generally omit the word nominal and just say interest rates) is due to changes in inflation. Real interest rates are determined by fundamental economic forces and move within a relatively tight range. Inflation rates are determined by government policies, which can vary dramatically. As inflation rates vary, so does expected inflation and, from Eq. (3.6), the level of nominal interest rates. Equation (3.6) explains what we see in Exhibit 3.5. It is also a warning that if inflation were to spike up from the current low rates of less than 2.0%, nominal interest rates would follow.

The foregoing observations are not limited to interest rates on Treasury securities. The forces that set equilibrium in the financial markets are real forces related to real rates of return. When inflation rises, investors will buy securities only if nominal expected returns rise by a comparable amount so that the expected real returns remain largely unchanged.

The foregoing points to an error often made by the financial media. They compare nominal rates of return over time. But given the variation in the rate of inflation documented in Exhibit 3.5, nominal rates should not be constant over time. Periods with higher inflation should have higher nominal returns on all assets. This is particularly true internationally where inflation rates can vary immensely. It is for this reason, unless otherwise noted, that we will specify whether real or nominal returns are used in making investment comparisons. That is a good habit to adopt.

BOND YIELDS AND BOND RETURNS

Let us set inflation aside for a moment to delve into the difference between bond yields and bond returns. We spent the whole first chapter stressing the importance of returns and have yet to mention them in our discussion of bonds. It turns out that the fact that bonds provided a fixed sequence of payments has implications for bond returns. The best way to see how it all operates is by working through a detailed example.

Consider an investor who buys a 10-year bond with a 3% coupon rate at a price of $100 dollars per $100 dollars in maturity value. When a bond sells for its maturity value it is said to be trading at par. The investor who purchases the bond will receive twenty semi-annual payments of $1.50 and a final principal payment of $100 for every $100 invested. To calculate the YTM, we need a more general version of Eq. (3.5). That more general version is given by Eq. (3.7), which relates the bond price, coupon, and YTM.

$$P = C_1/(1 + YTM/2) + C_2/(1 + YTM/2)^2$$
$$+ \cdots C^n/(1 + YTM/2)^n + Prin/(1 + YTM/2)^n \quad (3.7)$$

In Eq. (3.7), P is the price of the bond, the Cs are the semi-annual coupons, Prin is the principal paid at maturity, n is the maturity of the bond measured as the number of semi-annual periods, and YTM is the yield to maturity. Because the coupons and the principal are defined by the bond contract when a bond is issued, there are only two unknowns in Eq. (3.7): the price and the YTM. Although the equation is too complex to solve algebraically, a spreadsheet will quickly find the solution. Plugging in the 20 coupons of $1.50, the principal value of $100, and the price of $100 gives a YTM of 3.00%. That is not a fluke. In general, when a bond is selling at par the YTM equals the coupon rate.

Although we started with the price and solved for the YTM, that is not the way the bond market typically operates. Instead the level of yields in market is set by factors such as the level of macroeconomic activity, Federal Reserve policy, and particularly the rate of inflation. The price of a particular bond is then set so that its yield is equal to the general level of yields.

To continue the example, suppose that five years after the investor bought the bond, when it still has five years left to maturity, interest rates in the economy jump. New five-year bonds selling at par now carry a coupon rate of 5%. To remain competitive with the new bonds, the old bond must also offer a YTM of 5%. How does it do that? By selling for a lower price. Holding the coupon constant, as the price of a bond falls, the

YTM rises. For a five-year bond with a 3% coupon to have a yield of 5%, its price must be $91.25. At that price, the investor will earn 5% for the remaining five years. It may sound like that is too good to be true. The investor earns 3% for the first five years and 5% for the last five years on a 3% coupon bond purchased at par. The mistake is that the return for the first five years was not 3% because the investor experienced a capital loss. The investment of $100 is now worth only $91.25. Taking account of the capital loss the return over the first five years is actually only 1.30%.[2] As a result, the total return on the bond over the full 10 years is 3%, as it must be.

Exhibit 3.6 presents both the nominal and real returns on short-term Treasury bills and 20-year Treasury bonds over the period from 1960 to 2017. Notice that the Treasury bill nominal returns are never negative. Because the bills mature in a month, there is no opportunity for capital loss. The annual returns on the 20-year Treasury bonds are much more variable. This is because after one year a 20-year bond still has 19 years left until maturity. As a result, its price, and hence the investor return, depends on what has happened to yields on 19-year bonds in the past year. If market yields rise sharply, the bond price has to fall as it did in the example calculation. If the price drop is big enough, the annual return is negative. However, over the long run, coupon rates on new bonds adjust to reflect the new, higher interest rates. As a result, the average returns on 20-year Treasury bonds are higher, both in real and nominal terms, than those on Treasury bills, as they should be to reflect the risk associated with the greater price variation in the longer-term bonds.

---

[2]The return is calculated as twice the six-month internal rate of return to correspond with the yield to maturity convention.

EXHIBIT 3.6 Nominal and real treasury returns: 1960–2017.

Date	Treasury bill nominal returns (%)	Treasury bond nominal returns (%)	Treasury bill real returns (%)	Treasury bond real returns (%)
1960	2.58	13.32	1.21	10.47
1961	2.16	0.19	1.48	−1.93
1962	2.72	7.80	1.37	4.94
1963	3.15	−0.79	1.48	−3.82
1964	3.52	4.11	2.52	0.58
1965	3.96	−0.27	2.00	−4.07
1966	4.71	3.96	1.20	−0.71
1967	4.15	−6.02	1.08	−9.76
1968	5.29	−1.20	0.55	−6.16
1969	6.59	−6.52	0.37	−12.30
1970	6.38	12.69	0.77	5.93
1971	4.32	16.70	1.02	11.87
1972	3.89	5.15	0.47	1.21
1973	7.06	−2.49	−1.52	−8.92
1974	8.08	3.89	−3.79	−3.87
1975	5.82	6.10	−1.04	0.26
1976	5.16	18.18	0.28	12.39
1977	5.15	0.90	−1.45	−4.04
1978	7.31	−2.93	−1.57	−9.54
1979	10.69	−1.52	−2.30	−11.03
1980	11.52	−3.52	−0.88	−13.49
1981	14.86	1.16	5.45	−11.92
1982	10.66	39.74	6.58	26.28
1983	8.85	1.28	4.87	−6.95
1984	9.96	15.81	5.78	5.32
1985	7.68	31.96	3.74	22.56
1986	6.06	25.79	4.91	18.60
1987	5.38	−2.91	0.91	−7.87
1988	6.32	8.71	1.82	2.24
1989	8.22	19.23	3.41	10.18
1990	7.68	6.15	1.48	−1.43
1991	5.51	18.59	2.37	12.40
1992	3.40	7.95	0.49	4.40
1993	2.90	16.91	0.15	13.62
1994	3.88	−7.19	1.17	−10.66
1995	5.53	30.38	2.92	23.54
1996	5.14	−0.35	1.76	−5.22
1997	5.08	15.46	3.32	9.88
1998	4.78	13.05	3.12	7.89
1999	4.56	−8.66	1.83	−12.64
2000	5.76	20.95	2.29	14.37

EXHIBIT 3.6 (Continued)

Date	Treasury bill nominal returns (%)	Treasury bond nominal returns (%)	Treasury bill real returns (%)	Treasury bond real returns (%)
2001	3.78	4.09	2.19	0.30
2002	1.63	17.22	−0.73	15.33
2003	1.02	2.45	−0.85	1.42
2004	1.20	8.28	−1.99	7.00
2005	2.96	7.66	−0.44	4.56
2006	4.79	1.14	2.19	−3.48
2007	4.67	9.74	0.57	4.83
2008	1.47	25.60	1.38	23.78
2009	0.10	−13.99	−2.56	−14.07
2010	0.12	9.77	−1.35	9.64
2011	0.04	26.99	−2.84	26.94
2012	0.06	3.88	−1.66	3.82
2013	0.03	−12.23	−1.45	−12.26
2014	0.02	24.62	−0.73	24.59
2015	0.01	−0.67	−0.72	−0.68
2016	0.19	1.38	−1.85	1.19
2017	0.79	6.36	−1.32	4.25
Average full period	4.71	7.68	0.89	2.90
Average 1960–2007	5.55	7.76	1.30	2.14
Average 2008–2017	0.28	7.17	−1.31	6.72

TREASURY INFLATION PROTECTED SECURITIES (TIPS)

In addition to its nominal bonds, the U.S. Treasury also sells inflation-protected securities, or TIPS. These securities pay a fixed real rate of interest plus an added payment that compensates the investor for the realized rate of inflation. Consequently, the real rate that investors will earn on a TIPS is known, but the nominal rate is not because it depends on the subsequently realized inflation.

Because 10-year TIPS are relatively actively traded, comparing the yield on 10-year TIPS with the yield on 10-year nominal U.S.

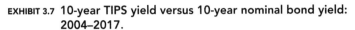

EXHIBIT 3.7 **10-year TIPS yield versus 10-year nominal bond yield: 2004–2017.**

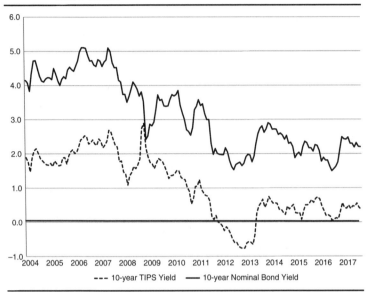

--- 10-year TIPS Yield   —— 10-year Nominal Bond Yield

Treasury bonds produces a measure of the bond market's expectation of inflation over the next 10 years. To illustrate, Exhibit 3.7 plots the yield on 10-year TIPS and 10-year nominal bonds over the period from 2004 to 2017. The first thing that jumps out from the exhibit is that in the years 2012 and 2013, the yield on the TIPS (the 10-year real interest rate) was negative. Investors who bought these bonds and held them to maturity were assured of experiencing a decrease in purchasing power. This does not mean that the nominal yield was negative, because the investors received an added payment based on the rate of inflation. Nonetheless, it is surprising that investors were willing to accept negative real rates.

The second thing to note is that for most of the period the gap between the nominal yield and the TIPS yield is around 2% – a bit more at the beginning and a bit less at the end. This implies that investors were generally expecting future inflation to be about 2% over the 10 years following the date on which the gap was observed. Such expectations are consistent with the forecasts of most major economic forecasting firms and with the Federal Reserve's inflation target. The exception to the rule is the period at the heart of the financial crisis in 2009, when the expected inflation fell to zero. This suggests that investors were fearing a prolonged recession that would eliminate inflation. When those fears diminished, inflation expectations returned to close to 2%. Finally, the exhibit clearly shows how nominal interest rates track expected inflation and that most of the variation in nominal rates is due to changes in expected inflation. This can be seen by noting that the gap between the two lines, which measures the expected rate of inflation, varies by a lot less than either of the individual lines.

Looking back at Exhibit 3.6, you can see that with an expected inflation rate of around 2%, the expected real returns on Treasury bills were negative throughout the period following the financial crisis. This pattern of expected negative real rates on short-term financial instruments has been due in large part to the aggressive financial policies of world central banks, including the Federal Reserve. It is anomalous by historical standards. For example, Exhibit 3.6 shows that prior to the financial crisis the average real return on Treasury bills over the period from 1960 to 2007 was 1.30%, whereas following the crisis in the years 2008 to 2017 the average real return was −1.32%.

These extraordinarily low real interest rates had two effects worth noting. One is that they made life difficult for savers. For example, living off retirement savings becomes a lot more difficult when the real return on fixed income securities is negative. This has led many savers to "reach for yield" by buying increasingly risky securities. Because the economy has remained solid since the end of the crisis, this strategy has not caused problems. But if another recession occurs, it could turn into a disaster for many savers. Second, the big beneficiary of the low rates has been the world's biggest debtor – the United States government. But there are storm clouds here as well. If interest rates return to more normal levels, it will become a good deal more difficult for the government to pay the interest on its massive and growing debt.

A look back at Exhibit 3.6 seems to contradict part of the story regarding low interest rates because the average real *return* on bonds in the years following the crisis is 6.99%, well above its long-run average of 2.14%. The answer to the apparent paradox is again changes in the prices of the long-term bonds. As interest rates declined, the capital gains on the bonds associated with the drop produced rising prices for long-term bonds. Those rising prices produced the high annual returns. That, however, is a one-time event. Once the prices of bonds adjust, future returns will be in line with the current nominal yields, which are about 2.5% for 20-year Treasury bonds.

CORPORATE BONDS AND CREDIT RISK

To this point, it has been assumed that all the promised payments made on a fixed income security will be paid. This is a reasonable assumption for Treasury securities because the government has the power to raise taxes and print money. It is also a reasonable assumption for highly successful companies like Apple, whose operating earnings far exceed the interest on the debt. However, it is not reasonable for many smaller and more financially stressed companies. For bonds issued by such companies, it is necessary to draw a distinction between the payments the company promises to make and the payments the investor actually expects to receive. This leads to a corresponding difference between the promised yield and the expected yield. Understanding the distinction is critical for investors considering holding riskier corporate bonds.

Like Treasury bonds, most corporate bonds are defined by four parameters: the par value, the coupon rate, the maturity, and the price. The first three parameters are set by the issuing company and are stated in the bond indenture. The final parameter is determined by the market. The price adjusts until the yield on the bond is competitive with other bonds of similar risk available in the market.

Virtually all corporate bonds follow several standard conventions. First, the par value to be repaid at maturity is $1,000. Second, coupons are paid semi-annually. As for Treasury bonds, the coupon payments equal the coupon rate times the par value divided by two. Third, bond prices are stated per hundred dollars of par value. Finally, dealers typically quote the bonds in terms of YTM.

PROMISED YIELDS VERSUS EXPECTED YIELDS

The yields to maturity we have been calculating so far are better described as promised yields. The YTM is the yield the investor will earn over the life of a bond *if* all the payments are made as promised. But as we expand the scope to consider borrowers who may not honor their commitment, a gap begins to open between the promised yield and the yield an investor actually expects to earn. This gap reflects the credit risk of the issuer. The less likely it is that the issuer will honor its commitments, the larger the gap.

If a company finds itself unable to honor its commitments as they come due, the normal solution is a restructuring of the company's financing either voluntarily or in the context of a formal bankruptcy. In a restructuring, it is generally the case the bondholders have to accept less than their promised payments. Given that investors recognize that borrowers who represent a credit risk may have to restructure, they will develop estimates of their expected yield that depend on the probability of a restructuring and the amount that they expect to recover if restructuring becomes necessary. The expected yield will be less than the promised yield because investors will take account of the possibility that interest and principal payments may be delayed or omitted.

The promised yield and the expected yield are both ex-ante measures, meaning that they are calculated before the bond matures or defaults. The actual return the investor earns over the course of an investment cannot be calculated until the bond has matured or restructured, so that all the cash payments are known. At that time, the actual return can be computed as the internal rate of return which discounts the stream of payments received to the purchase price of the bond. The actual return calculated in this fashion need not equal either the promised yield or the expected yield. For instance, a bond may have a promised yield of 8%, and an expected yield of 5%, but the actual yield may be only 1% because of an early default.

Bonds with credit risk can be thought of as being a hybrid between bonds without credit risk and equity. Like bonds without credit risk, the cash payouts on bonds with credit risk are limited by the fixed payments specified in the bond contract. They can never exceed the coupons and the principal. However, like equity, the actual yield earned on a bond with credit risk depends on the performance of the company. If the company does well and all the payments are made as promised, the investor reaps an unexpected windfall. On the other hand, if the company performs poorly and a restructuring is required, the investor will typically earn even less than the ex-ante expected yield.

Because of the importance of credit risk assessment to bond investors, an industry has grown up to provide bond ratings. Bond rating firms collect detailed financial data on issuers and analyze the information in order to sort bonds into ratings buckets. The two leading bond rating firms are Standard and Poor's and Moody's. The rating classifications used by Standard and Poor's run: AAA, AA, A, BBB, BB, B, CCC, CC, C, and D. The classifications used by Moody's has the same number of buckets but they are labeled slightly differently, as follows: Aaa, Aa, A, Baa, Ba, B, Caa, Ca, C, D.

By convention, bonds with a rating of BBB (or Baa) and above are considered to be investment grade. This cut-off is important because there are regulations that require some institutional bond-holders to limit their holdings to investment grade bonds. Bonds with a rating of BB or below are often referred to as "junk bonds" because of the risk of restructuring. Investment firms that deal in the bonds are not fond of that name. They prefer the label "high yield bonds" because the bonds have high promised yields. The two names, however, refer to the same thing. To avoid confusion, we will generally use the phrase "low grade" in the remainder of the book to refer to bonds with a rating below BBB.

As you might expect, as a bond's rating declines its promised yield rises to account for the fact that the ratings agencies believe that a restructuring is more likely. As evidence of this relation Exhibit 3.8 shows the promised yields on bonds by rating classification as of December 1, 2017. The data in the exhibit are from Merrill Lynch and refer to ratings by Standard & Poor's. As expected, the promised yields rise as the ratings fall from a low of 2.94% for AAA bonds, to 3.58% for BBB, to 5.83% for B, and all the way up to 10.76% for CCC. It bears repeating that the actual

EXHIBIT 3.8 Merrill Lynch U.S. corporate bonds.

Rating	Effective yield
AAA	2.94
AA	2.74
A	3.02
BBB	3.58
BB	4.29
B	5.83
CCC or below	10.76

earned yield spreads will be less than the promised spreads. The CCC promised yields are considerably higher than those for AAA bonds because the market believes the probability of restructuring is significant for such low-rated bonds.

Exhibit 3.8 shows the promised yields for bonds with different ratings at one point in time. However, spreads between the yields on high-grade bonds and low-grade bonds are far from constant over time. Exhibit 3.9 plots the spread between the yield on 10-year Treasury bonds and the promised yield on a diversified index of low-grade bonds maintained by Merrill Lynch. The index includes bonds with ratings from BB to CCC. What is most striking about the plot is how much the spread varies. During the height of the financial crisis the spread exceeded 20%. That means that lower-grade-bond issuers had to promise to pay yields approaching 25%! Clearly, investors did not expect to earn a 25% return. They demanded such a high promised yield because they felt there was a substantial probability of default. By 2017, the spread had dropped all the way to below 4%. Such a low spread implies that in 2017 investors believed the probability of default was a fraction of what it was during the crisis years.

Whereas promised yields and spreads can be observed directly, expected returns and expected spreads are unobservable.

EXHIBIT 3.9 Yield spread of low-grade bonds over 10-year Treasuries: 2007–2017.

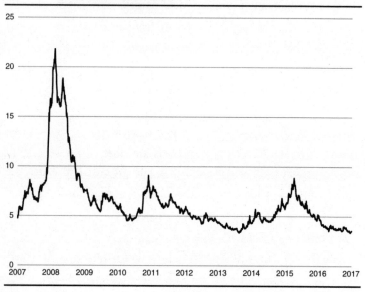

What investors expect to earn on a given bond depends on how likely they think restructuring is, how soon they believe a restructuring might occur, and what they can expect to receive in a restructuring. None of these are observable. However, by looking at history, we can get an estimate of the market's expected return spread compared to Treasuries. If investor expectations are fulfilled on average, then the historical average return spread will approximate the expected return spread. In the case of the Merrill Lynch low-grade-bond index, over the last 10 years the average return has been about 3% above the average return on Treasury bonds compared to an average promised yield spread of more than 5%. This means that losses due to restructurings averaged about 2% per year.

Exhibit 3.10 presents additional data, collected by Professor Edward Altman, on promised yield spreads compared to actual return spreads. Although the data are from an earlier period, they are still useful in illustrating the concepts. The data show high variation in the promised spread similar to that observed in more recent years. The return data are even more variable because of the impact of capital gains and losses. The exhibit shows that the average yield spread was 4.55%, whereas the average return spread was only 2.88%. The numbers are close to those reported for the Merrill Lynch Index. Whereas low-grade issues promise to pay rates about 5 percentage points over 10-year Treasury yields, investors end up earning about 3 percentage points above the returns on Treasuries because of restructurings.

Overall, the data suggest that a risk premium of about 3 percentage points fairly compensates investors for the risk in holding low-grade bonds. The promised yield is set so that after taking account of the probability of default, investors expect to earn an average rate of return 3 percentage points in excess of the yield on 10-year Treasury bonds.

THE ROLE OF DIVERSIFICATION IN BOND INVESTING

High-grade bonds of a given maturity are basically all alike. Because the payments they offer are fixed in advance, the only thing that can cause the price to move is a change in the level of interest rates. When interest rates change, bond prices adjust so that the yield on the bonds remains equal to the level of interest rates in the market as described in our previous example. Because all high-grade bonds will adjust in the same way, the risk reduction benefits of diversification are minimal.

EXHIBIT 3.10 **Altman data of yield spreads and return spreads: 1978–1999.**

Date	Promised yields (%)			Actual returns (%)		
	Low-grade bond yields	10-year Treasury yields	Spread	Low-grade bond returns	10-Year Treasury returns	Spread
1978	10.92	8.11	2.81	7.57	(1.11)	8.68
1979	12.07	9.13	2.94	3.69	(0.86)	4.55
1980	13.46	10.23	3.23	(1.00)	(2.96)	1.96
1981	15.97	12.08	3.89	7.56	0.48	7.08
1982	17.84	13.86	3.98	32.45	42.08	(9.63)
1983	15.74	10.70	5.04	21.80	2.23	19.57
1984	14.97	11.87	3.10	8.50	14.82	(6.32)
1985	13.50	8.99	4.51	26.08	31.54	(5.46)
1986	12.67	7.21	5.46	16.50	24.08	(7.58)
1987	13.89	8.83	5.06	4.57	(2.67)	7.24
1988	13.70	9.15	4.55	15.25	6.34	8.91
1989	15.17	7.93	7.24	1.98	16.72	(14.74)
1990	18.57	8.07	10.50	(8.46)	6.88	(15.34)
1991	12.56	6.70	5.86	43.23	17.18	26.05
1992	10.44	6.69	3.75	18.29	6.50	11.79
1993	9.08	5.80	3.28	18.33	12.08	6.25
1994	11.50	7.83	3.67	(2.55)	(8.29)	5.74
1995	9.76	5.58	4.18	22.40	23.58	(1.18)
1996	9.58	6.42	3.16	11.24	0.04	11.20
1997	9.20	5.75	3.45	14.27	11.16	3.11
1998	10.04	4.65	5.39	4.04	12.77	(8.73)
1999	11.41	6.44	4.97	1.73	(8.41)	10.14
Average	12.82	8.27	4.55	12.16	9.28	2.88

The same is not true of low-grade bonds. The returns on low-grade bonds depend not only on movements in interest rates but also on the financial performance of the issuer. One company may get in trouble and need to restructure, while another does well and makes all its payments as promised. If an investor holds a diversified portfolio of low-grade bonds, the bad results for some issues tend to be canceled by superior results for other issues.

As we explain in the next chapter, this reduces the risk of holding low-grade bonds.

SUPERIOR RETURNS FROM LOW-GRADE BOND INVESTING

There is one added aspect of investing in low-grade bonds that Michael Milken, the so-called "junk bond king," used to emphasize. Milken said: Suppose that you are a superior investor who can identify underpriced securities. If you find and buy an underpriced stock, you will not realize a big gain until the market recognizes the error of its ways and corrects the underpricing. As long as the stock stays underpriced, the investor does not make a superior return. Being right is not sufficient; the market has to come to realize that you are right. With a low-grade bond, on the other hand, being underpriced means the market has required a promised yield that is too large because it has overestimated the probability of restructuring. In your wisdom, you recognize that the company is not likely to restructure, and buy the bond. If you are right and the company does not restructure, you receive the promised payments, not the lower, market-expected payments. What is more, you get those higher payments whether or not the market ever comes to agree with you.

CONCEPTUAL FOUNDATION 3

The third conceptual foundation is that the ultimate goal of investing is to fund future consumption. Therefore, investment performance (returns) should be measured in real terms, not nominal terms. The dollar is not a good measure of value because it has been shrinking throughout most of American history.

Because sophisticated investors recognize that the dollar is shrinking, securities are priced so as to maintain the level of expected real returns. This is particularly clear in the case of fixed income securities which have predetermined promised yields. Those yields will move up and down with expected inflation so as to keep expected real returns relatively constant. The real return earned on a fixed income security depends on the rate of inflation that occurs during the life of the investment compared to the rate expected at the beginning.

4

RISK AND RETURN

Almost any investor will tell you that there is a trade-off between risk and return – to earn more return you have to bear more risk. Right? Not exactly. In fact, until the "risk" and "return" are defined more carefully the statement is at best largely vacuous. Worse still, it can be outright misleading.

First, bearing more risk does not necessarily lead to more return. If it did, investors would not really be bearing more risk because they could be assured of eventually getting a greater return. Instead, bearing more risk means it is more likely that you will suffer large losses. Second, all risks are not created equal. Consider betting $10,000 on the Superbowl. That is obviously risky for both you and your counterparty. But you can't both get more return from the risky bet. One person's win is the other's loss. Third, as we describe in detail below, some risks can be eliminated by diversification and others cannot. Should both types of risk be rewarded with the same return premium?

The scholars who developed the theory of asset pricing were aware of these issues. Part of their solution was to recognize that the theory only makes sense if you speak of *expected risk* and *expected return*. But already things are starting to get nebulous. Who is doing the expecting? This is not an idle question. Merton Miller tells a great story from the ceremonies at which he received his Nobel Prize in economics. As Miller recounts it,

> *I still remember the teasing we financial economists, Harry Markowitz, William Sharpe, and I, had to put up with from the physicists and chemists in Stockholm when we conceded that the basic unit of our research, the expected rate of return, was not actually observable. I tried to tease back by reminding them of their neutrino – a particle with no mass whose presence was inferred only as a missing residual from the interactions of other particles. But that was eight years ago. In the meantime, the neutrino has been detected.*

Unfortunately, unlike the neutrino expected returns have yet to be observed. So to better understand the alleged trade-off between risk and return, we have to go back to step one and define expected return more clearly. After that, we explore why bearing more expected risk should be rewarded with greater expected returns.

RISK AVERSION AND RISK PREMIUMS

Let's start with a thought experiment. Imagine that you stop at a freeway onramp and hand ten $100 bills to a bearded man holding a sign that says "homeless." Then imagine you give the same $1,000 to Bill Gates. Who do you think the gift will affect more? If you agree with economists, you will say the homeless man. A fundamental economic principle is the *declining marginal utility of wealth*. It sounds like a lot of jargon, but the idea is simple and important. The more wealth you have, the less enjoyment you get from each added dollar.

Economists formalize this idea with the concept of a utility function. The utility function measures the added happiness people receive from each dollar of additional consumable wealth. It is not a specific numeric function, but it is assumed to have two critical properties. First, utility (or happiness) increases as consumable wealth rises. This makes sense. Even if you have more money than you can spend in a lifetime, you can still get joy from starting a charitable foundation designed to make the world a better place (as Bill Gates is doing). Second, the increase in the utility you receive from an added dollar of consumable wealth falls as consumable wealth increases.[1]

An example of a utility function is shown in Exhibit 4.1. It is the shape of the function that is critical. The curve always rises but it does so at an ever-decreasing rate. Those properties are all you need to develop the notion of risk aversion and to understand why investors require added expected return for bearing added expected risk.

With that background, consider the opportunity to make a significant bet, say wagering $50,000 on the flip of a coin. Would you take the bet? The utility theory described above says no. Because the slope of the utility curve is always falling, the loss in utility associated with losing $50,000 exceeds the gain in utility associated with winning $50,000. To induce you to accept the bet, you would have

---

[1] For those of you who like the more terse calculus definition, the utility function is assumed to have a positive first derivative and a negative second derivative everywhere.

EXHIBIT 4.1 Typical utility function.

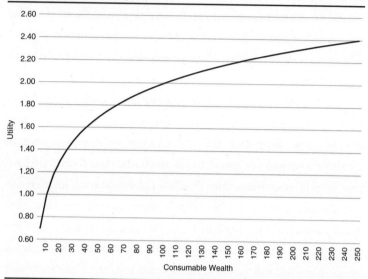

to be offered a risk premium. For example, you may take the bet if you win $75,000 if the coin lands heads, but lose only $50,000 if it lands tails. The size of the premium required to make you indifferent between accepting and rejecting the bet is a measure of your risk aversion. There is no reason to believe that all investors are equally risk averse, or even that the same individual is equally risk averse at different stages of life. Nonetheless, if most investors evidence some degree of risk aversion, security returns will embed risk premiums.

You might think that there is a clear counter example to this theory – Las Vegas. People go to Las Vegas and place bets where the expected outcome is negative, that is, where there is a negative risk premium, clearly contradicting the theory we just finished expounding. The economist answer to this is that gambling is form of entertainment and people are willing to pay for entertainment. The expected loss is the cost of the entertainment. However, there is a limit to how much fun people are willing to buy. When it comes to major financial decisions such as investing one's retirement fund or insuring one's house, economists believe that virtually all investors are risk averse.

But how do we know whether risk aversion affects financial markets? Is it true that risk premiums are impounded in asset prices? Is there a quick simple test for the hypothesis that investors must be offered a premium in the form of higher expected returns in order to purchase risky assets? The answer is yes, the hypothesis can be tested by comparing the long-run historical performance of different asset classes with different risks. While we don't know how to measure risk yet, take it on faith for the moment that stocks are riskier than long-term Treasury bonds, which in turn are riskier than short-term Treasury bills. If the market evidences risk aversion, then it follows that the expected return on stocks should exceed the expected return on bonds, which should in turn exceed the expected return on bills.

Unfortunately, as noted at the outset, the expected return, be it the market's expected return or any individual's expected return, is not directly observable. Nonetheless, if the expected return on stocks is greater than the expected returns on bonds and bills, then over the long run it should be observed that the average return on stocks is greater than the average return on bonds and bills.

Exhibit 4.2, which we first presented in Chapter 3, provides a test of the risk aversion hypothesis. It plots the real, inflation-adjusted paths of wealths (POWs) for the Center for Research in Securities Prices (CRSP) market index, 20-year U.S. Treasury bonds, and 30-day U.S. Treasury bills over the period from 1926 to 2017. It is important to note that we use real returns to calculate the POWs because consumable wealth must be measured in constant dollars.

The results are dramatic. An investment of $1 in 1926 grew to $406.54 inflation-adjusted dollars when invested in stocks, $10.34

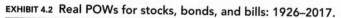

EXHIBIT 4.2 Real POWs for stocks, bonds, and bills: 1926–2017.

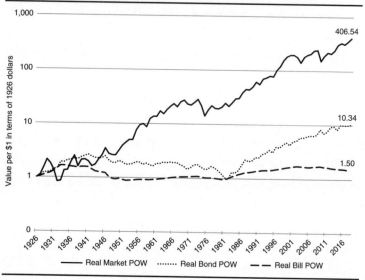

when invested in Treasury bonds, and only $1.50 when invested in Treasury bills. Note that the scale of the graph is logarithmic. Were that not the case, it would be hard to distinguish the POWs for bonds and bills from the x-axis during much of the period because their rate of appreciation is so much less than that of stocks. In a similar vein, Exhibit 4.3 reports the average real returns, both arithmetic and geometric, on stocks, bonds, and bills over the period. The geometric average real return on stocks is more than twice that on bonds and more than eight times that on bills. This is undisputable evidence that over the last century there has been a significant risk premium associated with investment in stocks compared to Treasury bills, and a smaller but still meaningful risk premium compared to investment in long-term Treasury bonds. Those premiums would not exist unless investors were risk averse, because risk-neutral investors would plunge into stocks and avoid Treasury securities until the expected return on all three

EXHIBIT 4.3 **Average return and volatility: 1926–2017.**

	Arithmetic average return (%)	Geometric average return (%)	Volatility (%)
Nominal			
CRSP market index	11.69	9.83	18.82
20-year Treasury bonds	5.97	5.54	9.82
30-day Treasury bills	3.39	3.34	3.14
ERP over bonds	5.72	4.30	21.66
Real			
CRSP market index	8.60	6.75	19.42
20-year Treasury bonds	3.12	2.57	10.84
30-day Treasury bills	0.51	0.44	3.78

instruments were the same. Over the last century, that has not happened.

The foregoing results, impressive as they are, still do not answer the question: What do we mean by expected return and expected risk? To address the deficiency, we start with expected return because that is easier. The concept is best illustrated by a simple example. Imagine an investment of $100 today that has three possible payoffs next year: $80 dollars with probability 0.25, $105 with probability 0.50 and $140 with probability 0.25. The expected payout is the probability-weighted average of all the possible outcomes. In this case that is

$$\text{Expected payout} = 0.25 * 80 + 0.50 * 105 + 0.25 * 140$$

$$= 107.5. \tag{4.1}$$

The expected return is, therefore,

$$\text{Expected return} = (107.5 - 100)/100 = 7.50\%.$$

Calculating the expected return is simple when you know the possible outcomes and their associated probabilities. Unfortunately, in the actual world of investments neither is observable. To make matters worse different investors may have different beliefs about both the possible outcomes and their probabilities. Finally, the "market's" expected return is some complicated weighted average of the expectations of all the investors in the market weighted by the amount they are willing to invest. Going forward, when we use the term "expected return," it will mean the market's expected return. This is standard in finance. It was the market's expected return that Prof. Miller was referring to at the Nobel ceremonies. The problem, as Miller observed, is that there are no objective data available on individual investors' expected returns, let alone the incredibly complicated combination of those expectations that make up the market expected return. Nonetheless, when the term "expected return" appears in finance articles it is almost always referring to the market expectation.

So how does it work in practice? What does it mean to speak of the market's expected return on Apple's stock? The idea is that somehow the market considers the future possible outcomes for Apple such as: whether the new iPhone will be successful; whether Apple services will grow rapidly; whether Apple will build a car; whether Apple will produce independent entertainment; and on and on. The market must estimate the possible payouts from all these uncertain businesses not only at one point in time as in our simple example, but at each year into the indefinite future.

The conceptual framework financial economists use to handle this situation is called "states of the world." Nature picks a state of the world and that determines *all* the contingencies in that state. This means, of course, that the number of states is massively large. Just to cover all the contingencies for Apple would require an immense number of states and the states have to cover all the contingencies for every company. But if you could describe all the states and assign a probability to each, the expected return could be calculated directly. Unfortunately, that is a huge if. Given the immense number of states and given that there is no known way of estimating the probabilities for each state, the model is a beautiful theoretical formulation of little practical value.

Instead, the practical solution is to assume that somehow the market has reduced all the complexity of the states into a series of annual expected cash flows. That is, for each future year the market has done a calculation akin to that shown by Eq. (4.1). With this series of expected future cash flows, and an estimate of their risk (we will get to risk shortly), the market sets the current price of Apple so that an investor who buys the stock and receives rights to a pro rata share of the cash flows can expect to earn a rate of return that fairly compensates for the risk of holding Apple.

Admittedly, the whole framework appears remarkably abstract, nebulous, and untestable, so you can see why physicists tease financial economists.[2] There is, however, a path forward related to our discussion of stocks, bonds, and bills. Although expected returns are not observable, past returns are. If we can come up with a measure of risk, then it would be possible to examine whether riskier securities have provided greater past average returns. That is the path that research in finance has followed.

The phrase "risk–return trade-off" seems to imply that if an investor bears risk he or she will be rewarded with greater expected returns, but that is not the case. It is not risk per se that warrants a premium, it is economic risk that cannot be avoided or eliminated by diversification. First, with regard to avoidable risks, most gambling falls into this category. As noted earlier, if my friend and I bet on a football game, we both bear risk but we can't both earn risk premiums. So who gets the premium? The answer is neither

---

[2] In defense of financial economists, dark energy appears to have much in common with expected return.

of us. The risk can be entirely avoided by just not betting on the game. This is not a risk that society must bear as part of ongoing economic activity.

In this respect, buying Apple stock is different. Apple requires investors to provide it with financing as part of its operation. Therefore, the risk of holding Apple stock is not a risk that can be avoided. Someone must bear the risk if we are to have our iPhones. This makes it sound like the volatility of Apple stock would be the appropriate measure of risk, but that too is wrong. Investors do not have to bear all of that risk, because of diversification.

To appreciate the impact of diversification, consider the risk of fire damage that homeowners face. For millions of homeowners nationwide this is clearly a risk that cannot be avoided. Typically homeowners are unwilling to bear the risk, so they transfer the risk to insurance companies in the form of a homeowner's policy. From this it seems to follow that the insurance companies should receive a substantial premium for bearing the risk. And while insurance companies do earn a premium, it is much smaller than you would guess based on the risk that individual homeowners face. The reason the premium is small is because insurance companies can drastically reduce the risk by diversifying across hundreds of thousands of policies.

To see more fully how diversification works, consider the following thought experiment. Imagine you are an insurance company and you have agreed to make a payment to policy holders based on the extent to which the fraction of heads in a series of coin flips differs from 50%. If the coin is only flipped once, the insurance company is going to have to make a big payment because the observed fraction will either 0 or 1 – not close to 50%. But as the number of flips increases, the probability that the observed fraction is close to 50% rises. For one million flips, the probability that the fraction will be between 49.9% and 50.1% is 0.99. In other words, virtually all of uncertainty the hypothetical insurance company faces has been eliminated by diversification. The company can be highly confident that it will not have to make a large payment. Fire insurance works the same way. By insuring hundreds of thousands of different houses around the country, an insurance company can estimate with remarkable accuracy what fraction will burn each year. The insurance company does not know which specific houses will burn, but that does not matter. The amount the insurance company will have to pay depends only on the fraction of a large number of policies that have claims. And that number is highly predictable. Therefore, the insurance company bears little risk and does not require a large risk premium.

The same is true of investors. If an investor poured every penny of his or her portfolio into Apple stock, then the risk of variation in his or her consumable wealth would be highly dependent on Apple stock. But rational investors don't do that. They hold diversified portfolios. Because stocks returns are not perfectly correlated, on days when Apple drops, Coke might rise. A well-diversified portfolio will have lots of winners and losers that will tend to cancel each other. As a result, the volatility of the portfolio is typically less than that of its individual constituents and it is the volatility of the overall portfolio that determines the risk of consumable wealth, not the volatility of the individual components. Therefore, an individual holding, like Apple, is risky only to the extent that it adds to the risk of the entire portfolio. That insight was first developed mathematically by William Sharpe, who received the Nobel Prize for his work on the Capital Asset Pricing Model, CAPM. (Yes this is the same Bill Sharpe of Sharpe's arithmetic.)

We leave the details on the derivation of the CAPM to investment textbooks. However, the final result is so important that it merits attention. Mathematically, the CAPM as applied to Apple, says

$$E(r_{Apple}) - r_f = Beta_{Apple} * [E(r_{market}) - r_f]. \quad (4.2)$$

In words, Eq. (4.2) says that the expected risk premium associated with holding Apple's stock equals the expected market risk premium (often called the equity risk premium) times the Beta of Apple's stock. Beta can be thought of as a magnification factor. The market portfolio has a Beta of 1.0 – it cannot magnify itself. Stocks with Betas greater than one magnify market movements, stocks with Betas less than one shrink market movements. In the context of the CAPM, the only risk that cannot be eliminated through diversification is the risk in the overall movement in the market. It therefore makes perfect sense that the risk premium for Apple is proportional to Apple's Beta because that Beta measures the extent to which Apple's stock price movements magnify the market movements and the market is the sole source of non-diversifiable (often called systematic) risk.

In the years since its development, there have been hundreds of tests of the CAPM and many of them have found it wanting. The main deficiency the tests point to is the market being the only source of systematic risk. But the idea that only systematic risk is rewarded with premiums remained unscathed. The question has become: What are the sources of systematic risk other than movements in the market portfolio?

In an influential paper, Eugene Fama and Kenneth French presented evidence which indicated that a three-factor model produced a more accurate description of average returns across stocks than the CAPM. Unlike Prof. Sharpe, however, Fama and French did not derive their model from first principles. The two additional factors they added, one based on market capitalization and one based on the performance of value stocks compared to growth stocks, were included because they worked. This led researchers to think that they might be able to find other factors that worked better than the Fama–French factors and the race was on. In a paper published in 2016, Harvey, Liu, and Zhu surveyed 313 academic papers that addressed the problem of finding the best risk factors. The authors reported that by 2016 the total number of factors used to explain risk premiums on stocks had exploded to 316. Those factors ran the gauntlet from the rate of inflation, to firm profitability, to firm distress, and everything in between.

What is the takeaway from all this? First, and most importantly, there is agreement on the two basic points. Risk premiums should not be associated with risks that can be avoided or eliminated through diversification. Premiums should only be paid for bearing systematic risks. Second, it is also agreed that the movements in the overall stock market is one systematic risk factor. Unfortunately, after that the consensus collapses. What the other risk factors are remains an area of dispute.

What is done in practice? The most common solution is to use the CAPM. The model may have its deficiencies but it is easy to understand and apply. Furthermore, it typically gives estimates of risk premiums that are not unreasonable. In addition, the CAPM measure of risk, the Betas, are widely available. For instance, they are reported by both Yahoo Finance and Google Finance. But like everything else in finance they are estimates and estimates depend on how the estimation is done. Apple is the world's largest company by market capitalization; it is also one of the most widely followed and actively traded companies in the world. If any stock should have a precise Beta it would be Apple. Nonetheless, as of this writing Google is reporting that Apple has a Beta of 1.25 and Yahoo is reporting that Apple's Beta is 1.40. For Tesla, Yahoo reports a Beta of 0.73, well less than the market portfolio's Beta of 1.00. Google's estimate, on the other hand, is 0.98. This type of variation is not unique. Because of the difficulties with accurately estimating Beta, Spanish financial economist Pablo Fernandez argues that investors are better off simply assuming that all stocks have the same Beta of 1.0 as the overall market. This position is extreme, but investors should be aware that Beta is not something like the speed of light that is unchanging and can be measured with precision.

Once you have settled on a Beta, the CAPM still does not provide a numerical answer for the risk premium on a stock. Looking back, Eq. (4.2) says that Apple's risk premium should equal Apple's Beta times the risk premium for the market (the equity risk premium). This means that to estimate the expected return on any stock you must first come up with an estimate of the equity risk premium.

Aside from its use in the CAPM, the equity risk premium, henceforth referred to as the ERP, is critically important in financial planning. For instance, a typical retirement fund holds a combination of stocks and bonds. The yield on bonds can be calculated directly, but what about stocks? If the investor holds the market portfolio, which has a Beta equal to 1.0, the expected return is the current yield on government bonds plus the equity risk premium. As a result, the amount of money a pension fund must contribute to finance its retirement liabilities depends on an estimate of the equity risk premium. The higher the assumed ERP, the lower the required funding. This has made the ERP a political football because cash-strapped states and municipalities want to minimize the payments they have to make to fund defined contribution pension plans. The problem is that if assumptions regarding the ERP are overly optimistic, so that actual returns fall short of the assumptions, the fund may be unable to pay benefits as they come due. All this raises the question: What is a reasonable estimate of the ERP?

THE EQUITY MARKET RISK PREMIUM

The ERP is the added return that investors can expect from investing in stocks compared to investing in Treasury bonds. Pricing models like the CAPM cannot be used to estimate the ERP, because it is an input into the model. The place to start is with the historical track record. A look back at Exhibit 4.3 shows that the arithmetic average difference between CRSP index returns and Treasury bond returns was 5.72%, whereas the geometric average difference was 4.30%. This suggests that the equity risk premium should be around 5% to make investors indifferent between stocks and Treasury bonds.

Using an historical average to estimate the forward-looking equity risk premium is valid only if the unobservable expected risk premium has remained constant over time. But that assumption is almost certainly false. There are a host of reasons why the equity risk premium is likely to have *declined* over time. Those reasons include the following:

1. Increases in market liquidity along with improvements in trading technology and record keeping.
2. Innovations in capital market regulation and oversight to protect investors including the establishment of the Securities Exchange Commission.
3. Advances in economic theory and policy leading to increased stabilization of the economy.

4. Advances in asset pricing and portfolio theory leading to improved risk measurement and investment management.

5. The expansion of stock market participation via the invention of mutual funds, exchange traded funds, and the creation of the modern retirement savings system.

6. The collection and dispersion of data on the financial performance of equity investments leading to, among other things, investor appreciation that equities are not exotic investments with an unacceptable level of risk.

7. A decline in the volatility of the return on the market portfolio.

8. An aging of the U.S. population, who will likely sell equities to fund retirement reducing expected market returns.

Given the likelihood that the expected risk premium has declined over the last 90 years, an historical average will be an upward-biased estimate of the forward-looking risk premium.

Aware of the potential biases inherent in the use of historical averages, particularly those based exclusively on U.S. data, academics and practitioners have turned to other approaches for estimating the equity risk premium. One of the most widely accepted is the discounted cash flow model applied to the market as a whole.[3] Given the current observable price index for the market (for instance, the S&P 500 is at 2604 as we write this) and predictions regarding future dividends on the stocks in the index, we can calculate the discount rate that equates the present value of the dividends to the index. This discount rate is by definition the expected rate of return for the market index. Subtracting the

---

[3] DCF models are discussed in more detail in Chapter 5.

yield on Treasury bonds produces an estimate of the ERP. Prof. Aswath Damodaran publishes on his website a monthly time series of forward-looking equity risk premiums. His most current estimate, for December 2016, is approximately 5.7%, calculated with respect to the yield on 10-year government bonds. Had he used 20-year bonds, his estimate would have been 5.5%. It is comforting that this estimate is not too different from that based on historical data.

All of the foregoing considerations apply to U.S. data. It is common for analysts to rely on U.S. data because they are the most complete and the most accurate. But that itself is a problem. The U.S. data are so complete and clean because during the last century, the United States became the world's leading economy. During that time, the United States was politically stable, it did not lose a war, and it had the most rapidly growing financial markets. For all of those reasons, the historical U.S. data are likely to be biased. From the perspective of 1926, investors would have had no reason to believe that the U.S. would be blessed over the next 91 years. To overcome this bias, Dimson, Marsh, and Staunton (2002) look at stock market returns on a global basis throughout the twentieth century.[4] They conclude that historical averages based on U.S. data likely overstate the forward-looking equity risk premium. They suggest that an ERP of around 4% is more appropriate.

Finally, there is the question of how to compute the average premium. If annual returns are uncorrelated over time, and the goal is to estimate the risk premium for next year, the arithmetic average is the best estimate. There is evidence, however, that stock returns are negatively correlated over time. If so, the arithmetic average will tend to overstate the future premium. Second, in an

---

[4]Elroy Dimson, Paul Marsh, and Mike Staunton (2002). *Triumph of the Optimists: 101 Years of Global Investment Returns*. Princeton, NJ: Princeton University Press.

investment context the goal is typically to estimate the average premium over a longer horizon (generally of the order of 5–10 years). Over such longer horizons, the geometric average is likely to be a better choice.

In light of the foregoing, it is not surprising that there is still an active debate regarding the appropriate estimate of the forward-looking equity risk premium. For the remainder of this book, we take a middle-of-the-road position and use 5.0%.

APPLYING THE CAPM

To provide some hands-on feeling for how the CAPM works, it is applied to 12 well-known companies on November 28, 2017 in Exhibit 4.4. The Betas in the exhibit are all taken from Google. To put the Betas in perspective, remember that the Beta for the market portfolio is 1.0. Based on the intuitive description of Betas as factors that magnify market moves, the estimates in Exhibit 4.4 make sense. At the low end of the scale are the Betas for companies whose businesses depend less on the vagaries of the overall

EXHIBIT 4.4 CAPM expected returns as of November 28, 2017.

Company	Beta	20-year Treasury yield (%)	ERP (%)	Expected return (%)
Amazon	1.45	2.58	5.00	9.83
Apple	1.25	2.58	5.00	8.83
Berkshire Hathaway	0.87	2.58	5.00	6.93
Edison International	0.24	2.58	5.00	3.78
General Electric	1.11	2.58	5.00	8.13
General Motors	1.56	2.58	5.00	10.38
Hubspot	2.40	2.58	5.00	14.58
JP Morgan	1.22	2.58	5.00	8.68
Merck	0.78	2.58	5.00	6.48
Netflix	1.39	2.58	5.00	9.53
Proctor and Gamble	0.66	2.58	5.00	5.88
Exxon	0.83	2.58	5.00	6.73

economy, such as Exxon, and Proctor and Gamble, and especially Edison International, whose Beta is only 0.20. It turns out that people buy electricity, at largely regulated prices, in good times and bad. At the high end, technology companies, particularly small, young ones like HubSpot, have high Betas. But even large technology companies like Apple and Amazon have Betas greater than 1.0. GM's Beta of 1.56, higher than that of Amazon, is a bit surprising. This could reflect the fact that car purchases are sensitive to economic conditions, but it could also be the result of measurement error. Finally, large diversified companies that tend to mirror the overall economy, such as Berkshire Hathaway and General Electric, have Betas near 1.0 as expected.

Given the current yields on 20-year Treasury bonds, and an ERP of 5%, the expected returns for the sample of stocks in Exhibit 4.4 range from 5.88% for Edison to 14.58% for HubSpot. This range covers more than 95% of all listed stocks. Note that the expected returns will vary from day to day as the yield on 20-year Treasury bonds changes. In principle, the Beta could change too, but because it cannot be measured with precision, the extent of such short-term variation is unknown.

APPLYING THE CAPM TO SECURITIES OTHER THAN STOCKS

The CAPM can be applied to securities other than common stocks. Low-grade bonds provide an example. In Chapter 3, we noted that low-grade bonds are a hybrid security. Like high-grade bonds they promise periodic fixed payouts. Unlike high-grade bonds, the probability of the company actually honoring those promises depends on business conditions. In that sense, the securities are more like equities. We also noted a problem with low-grade bonds. Although the promised yield on the bonds could be calculated directly, there was no specified procedure, other than using historical averages, for estimating the expected return. The CAPM solves that problem.

It turns out the Beta for low-grade bonds is of the order of 0.50 with lower-rated bonds having higher Betas. Using the Treasury bond yield of 2.58% and the equity risk premium of 5.00% from Exhibit 4.4, a Beta of 0.50 corresponds to an expected return of 5.08% and a risk premium of 2.5%. Those numbers are close to the historical averages presented in Chapter 3.

DISCOUNT RATES FOR EQUITY CASH FLOWS

Expected returns are also the proper discount rate for calculating the present value of equity cash flows like dividends. Discounting is an issue we address in detail in the next chapter. In the case of equities, the expected return is the proper discount rate because it is what the market judges to be a fair risk-adjusted return. Suppose, for example, that you expect to get $1 in a dividend next year from a company and the CAPM expected return for the company is 10%. Remember this is an expected payout, not a sure thing. In order for your expected return to be 10%, the current value of the payout must be,

$$\text{Current value} = \$1.00/(1 + 0.10). \qquad (4.3)$$

To see this, use the definition of return,

$$\text{Return} = (\$1.00 - \text{Current value})/\text{Current value}.$$

Plugging in the current value from Eq. (4.3) and simplifying gives

$$\text{Return} = 10\%.$$

This demonstrates that the expected return is the proper discount rate.

These discount rates play a key role in estimating the fundamental value of common stock as we shall see in the next chapter.

LIQUIDITY AND EXPECTED RETURNS

Although risk is the primary determinant of expected returns, it is not the only determinant. Of all the other factors, liquidity is the most important. Defining liquidity is not straightforward. This is an issue we discuss in greater depth in Chapter 9. For now, the liquidity of a financial asset can be taken as measured by the volume of the security that can be sold without taking a significant haircut from the current market price.

Liquidity clearly has value to investors. Being able to convert a financial asset to cash immediately at the current market price provides investors with a type of insurance. In the event of a sudden development, highly liquid financial assets can be sold at current prices to meet a contingency such as a health crisis. Because of the value conveyed by liquidity, investors should be willing to accept lower expected returns on more liquid assets and that is what the research finds. The benefits of liquidity are easiest to detect in the case of Treasury securities. Because the payouts on Treasury securities are specified and free from default risk, their future returns can be computed with precision. It turns out that even in the Treasury market, where all securities are highly liquid, the most liquid securities, which turn out to be those that were most recently issued, trade at slightly lower yields.

In the case of common stock, the impact of liquidity is much more difficult to assess. Unlike Treasury securities, the expected return on common stock cannot be measured with precision because of the volatility of stock prices. This makes is more difficult to say that one stock has a higher expected return than another. To further complicate the issue, the differences in liquidity, unlike differences in risk, are likely to be small because of the efficiency of modern trading technology. This means it would take a very long sample period to determine whether the expected return for one stock was greater than for another due to liquidity. But over long periods of time both the risk and liquidity of the stock may change, rendering study results a meaningless mix of apples and oranges.

As a practical matter, from the standpoint of most investors, virtually all actively traded stocks are nearly completely liquid. Individual investors can trade all they want within a whisker of the market price at the push of a button. In the case of publicly traded common stocks, liquidity is an issue that can be safely ignored.

Where liquidity starts to become important is when alternative assets such as real estate and private company equity are considered. One would expect that these assets command higher expected returns to compensate for the illiquidity, but it is difficult to quantify. For instance, data on the trading history of private company shares are both scarce and sporadic. There is nothing akin to the daily closing price that exists for publicly traded shares. As a result, while it is widely agreed that such assets would offer meaningful illiquidity premiums, their magnitude remains an active area of research and dispute.

CONCEPTUAL FOUNDATION 4

The risk–return trade-off is one of the key conceptual foundations of finance and investing, but it is not what it appears at first sight. Bearing more risk does not mean getting higher returns. It does not even mean you can expect higher returns. Some risks are not compensated at all. The actual trade-off is between expected return and expected systematic risk. Systematic risks are those risks that cannot be avoided or eliminated via diversification. Though there remains a great deal of debate regarding the precise way to measure systematic risk, it is agreed that one aspect of that risk is the sensitivity of a stock's return to variation in returns on the market portfolio as measured by the stock's Beta. Which additional systematic risk factors may be relevant is the subject of ongoing research.

5

FUNDAMENTAL ANALYSIS AND VALUATION

There are two fundamentally different approaches to active investing. One is to buy securities that you believe are well-priced relative to the future cash flows you expect to receive as an owner. If your belief is correct and if you hold the security long enough, either the cash you receive will justify the purchase and/or eventually the market will come to appreciate the value of the security, giving you the opportunity to sell at a price that produces a superior return. The second approach is to buy a security with the intent of reselling it in the relatively near future at a higher price. Much technical analysis is based on the second approach. Charts are analyzed with the goal of identifying when prices will rise or fall so as to profit from the price movement. Security cash flow is largely irrelevant. The goal is to buy today what you think someone will pay more for tomorrow.

The effort to buy assets you think someone will pay more for tomorrow is not something we address in this book. It falls more into the realm of psychology than finance. Therefore, we do not see it as a fundamental concept of investing. There is, however, one aspect of the buy low/sell high approach that is worth addressing before we leave the topic and that is the possibility of bubbles.

BUBBLES

If a sufficient number of traders employ the buy low/sell high strategy, it is possible for price increases to become self-fulfilling. Investors buy today because prices have risen in the past. Their purchases push prices up further, thereby reinforcing the belief that the price will rise in the future. As long as there are enough new buyers with sufficient funds to invest, prices can rise for an extended period without there being any fundamental reason for the increase. This is what is called a bubble.

Perhaps the most famous example of a bubble is the tulipomania that occurred in Holland in the sixteenth century. Before the bubble popped, the price of tulip bulbs rose by a factor of more than 20 in less than two years. While it is true that tulip bulbs have some fundamental value because they can be planted to grow tulips, there is no reason why that fundamental value should suddenly jump by a factor of more than 20. In fact, during the height of the boom fewer bulbs were planted because they were being held for resale.

Lest you think that such an event could never happen today, consider the case of Bitcoin. Bitcoins are an electronic currency that can be held without the risk of expropriation or theft through an ingenious technology known as blockchain.[1] Bitcoins do not

---

[1] Bitcoin can be hacked at the trading stage before it is entered into the blockchain, so there is risk of theft at that stage.

now, nor will they ever, pay a dividend. They are also difficult to use as a means of exchange for normal purchases because few merchants accept them and because their value is so volatile. Therefore, owning Bitcoins does not convey much in the way of benefits other than the possibility of selling them at a higher price in the future. But that apparently is enough because the rise in the price of Bitcoins has been phenomenal.

Monthly data on the prices of a Bitcoin are presented in Exhibit 5.1 for the period January 2013 through December 2017. In less than five years, the price of a coin rose from $20 to $15,749.00, a compound annual growth rate of 430%! But the recent rise has been even more spectacular. During 2017, Bitcoin rocketed up 1,530%! This price explosion occurred despite the fact that Bitcoins in 2017 were essentially identical to coins in 2013. They still paid no dividend and were difficult to use for normal transactions. Given these facts, it is hard to explain such a massive price increase as anything other than a self-reinforcing bubble. Prices rose because people expected them to rise. Furthermore, the rise was so dramatic that people with little knowledge of financial markets, such as our barber, began investing so as to avoid missing out on the boom.

The greatest risk of bubbles is that they can pop and prices can drop dramatically. After rising for years, tulip bulb prices in Holland collapsed back to their original level in less than three months. The problem is that if the main source of demand is the general expectation of higher future prices, as soon as prices stop rising, demand evaporates. With few, if any, buyers willing to purchase on the basis of the security's fundamental value, prices collapse. We suspect this will happen to Bitcoin. In that regard, John Bogle, the legendary founder of Vanguard, perhaps said it best. When the price of Bitcoin roared past $10,000 he

EXHIBIT 5.1 Bitcoin prices: January 2013–December 2017.

Date	Bitcoin price	Bitcoin return
Jan-13	20	
Feb-13	33	65.00%
Mar-13	93	181.82%
Apr-13	139	49.46%
May-13	129	−7.19%
Jun-13	97	−24.81%
Jul-13	98	1.03%
Aug-13	129	31.63%
Sep-13	123	−4.65%
Oct-13	198	60.98%
Nov-13	1112	461.62%
Dec-13	728	−34.53%
Jan-14	800	9.89%
Feb-14	565	−29.38%
Mar-14	452	−20.00%
Apr-14	448	−0.88%
May-14	635	41.74%
Jun-14	640	0.79%
Jul-14	579	−9.53%
Aug-14	483	−16.58%
Sep-14	387	−19.88%
Oct-14	337	−12.92%
Nov-14	376	11.57%
Dec-14	317	−15.69%
Jan-15	217	−31.55%
Feb-15	256	17.97%
Mar-15	244	−4.69%
Apr-15	236	−3.28%
May-15	229	−2.97%
Jun-15	263	14.85%
Jul-15	284	7.98%
Aug-15	231	−18.66%
Sep-15	236	2.16%
Oct-15	316	33.90%
Nov-15	376	18.99%
Dec-15	429	14.10%
Jan-16	365	−14.92%
Feb-16	439	20.27%
Mar-16	416	−5.24%
Apr-16	446	7.21%
May-16	530	18.83%
Jun-16	674	27.17%
Jul-16	623	−7.57%

EXHIBIT 5.1 (Continued)

Date	Bitcoin price	Bitcoin return
Aug-16	576	−7.54%
Sep-16	611	6.08%
Oct-16	704	15.22%
Nov-16	739	4.97%
Dec-16	966	30.72%
Jan-17	966	0.00%
Feb-17	1189	23.08%
Mar-17	1081	−9.08%
Apr-17	1435	32.75%
May-17	2191	52.68%
Jun-17	2420	10.45%
Jul-17	2856	18.02%
Aug-17	4718	65.20%
Sep-17	4367	−7.44%
Oct-17	6458	47.88%
Nov-17	10757	66.57%
Dec-17	15749	46.41%
Arithmetic average		838.04%
Geometric average	430%	
For 2017	1530%	

quipped, "Bitcoin may well go to $20,000 but that won't prove I'm wrong. When it gets back to $100, we'll talk."

There is often debate regarding whether a price increase represents a bubble. In the case of Bitcoin, the evidence is strong in our view. Because Bitcoin is a marginal currency that offers no cash payout of any sort, it has essentially no fundamental value. Consequently, it is hard to attribute the dramatic price increase shown in Exhibit 5.1 to anything other than a self-reinforcing bubble. In the case of common stock, the waters are murkier. Stocks convey rights to current and future distributions and, as such, always have some fundamental value. During stock market booms, a question often arises regarding the extent to which the price increases are due to reasonable projections of improving fundamentals as opposed to the impact of a self-reinforcing bubble. For instance, to this day a debate remains as to whether the boom and collapse of technology stock prices during the dot.com era was the result of a bubble or of reasonable growth expectations that were not fulfilled. Most practitioners accept the bubble explanation, but not all academics are convinced.

To provide perspective, Exhibit 5.2 plots the monthly progression of the NASDAQ index from January of 1997 to September of 2001. During the first three years and two months, the Index rose by an astonishing 370%, only to have almost the entire gain erased in the next 18 months. Given the dramatic rise and fall during a period when aggregate economic activity changed

EXHIBIT 5.2 NASDAQ index: January 1997–September 2001.

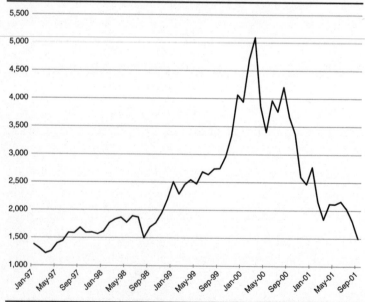

very little, many financial economists have concluded that the episode was an example of a bubble. However, there are hold-outs who argue that the run-up was based on rational assessments of future business prospects that were not subsequently realized. If investors are willing to accept sufficiently optimistic projections regarding future profits based on assumptions of revolutionary new business models, then it is possible to justify sky-high values on the basis of "fundamentals." After all, Amazons do occur. After the revolution fails to materialize, those who predicted it are often ridiculed, but that does not mean their beliefs were irrational at the time.

To illustrate how difficult it is to distinguish bubble-like behavior from rational beliefs regarding future revolutionary business innovation in real time, consider the case of Tesla. Exhibit 5.3

EXHIBIT 5.3 GM benchmark versus Tesla: January 2012–July 2017.

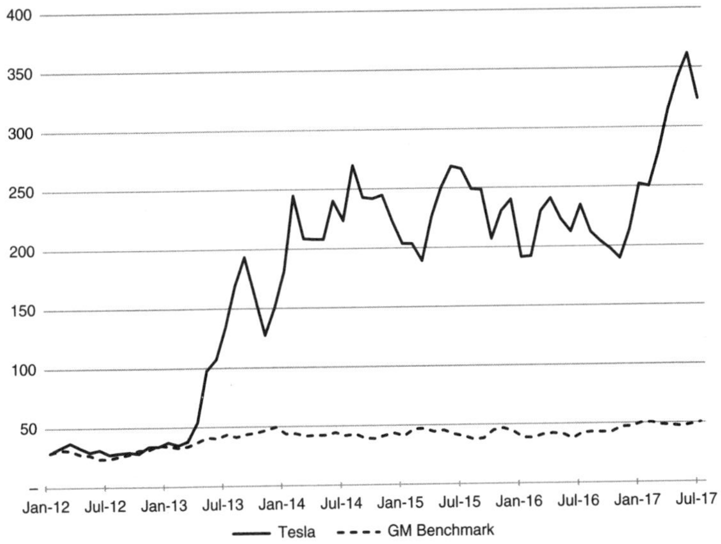

plots the price of Tesla's stock against a benchmark path of wealth (POW) derived from the returns on GM stock.[2] For the first 14 months the two series move together as one might expect for two car companies. Then, following the introduction of the Tesla model S, the two lines begin to diverge. Over the next four years Tesla increases by nearly 1,000%, while the GM benchmark rises only marginally. At one point in 2017, the stock market capitalization of Tesla passed that of GM, even though Tesla had only a small fraction of GM's revenue. Furthermore, Tesla was not profitable at the time and had significant negative free cash flow. Does this mean that the run-up in Tesla's stock was due, at least in part, to a bubble? At SMBP we thought it was, but many others did not. Because SMBP was taking a position on the stock (we discuss the position later in the chapter), we followed the analyst reports and the Internet chatter. Some well-known analysts felt that the stock was still a bargain even at its peak. On the Internet, the company and its leader, Elon Musk, were lauded for what many claimed was a total disruption of the automobile industry. In their view, this was not a bubble but a rational response to the next Amazon or Apple. As we write this, the jury is still out on who was right.

The experience of Tesla is not unique. As we write this, Netflix is trading at a price/earnings multiple of 228 and Amazon at a multiple of 359. To be sure these are both wonderful, innovative companies and also Amazon is protected by significant barriers to entry. But is that enough to explain the sky-high prices relative to earnings? Does it suggest that there might be an element of Bitcoin in such extraordinary valuations? Unfortunately, there is no general procedure for determining whether the price of a

---

[2] Because GM pays a dividend, it is necessary to construct a GM POW to compare it to Tesla, which does not pay a dividend.

stock reflects bubble behavior or not. It depends on the facts and circumstances of the individual case. In our view, investors are well advised to limit their purchases to securities whose value they can rationalize on the basis of a fundamental analysis of the type we describe in the next section. The risks of being seduced into trying to guess future price movements based on their past gyrations are the risks of a foolhardy game. In that respect, no one has said it better than Warren Buffett, who offered a wonderful analogy in his 2013 letter to Berkshire shareholders. Mr. Buffett said,

> It should be an enormous advantage for investors in stocks to have those wildly fluctuating valuations placed on their holdings – and for some investors, it is. After all, if a moody fellow with a farm bordering my property yelled out a price every day to me at which he would either buy my farm or sell me his – and those prices varied widely over short periods of time depending on his mental state – how in the world could I be other than benefited by his erratic behavior? If his daily shout-out was ridiculously low, and I had some spare cash, I would buy his farm. If the number he yelled was absurdly high, I could either sell to him or just go on farming.
>
> Owners of stocks, however, too often let the capricious and often irrational behavior of their fellow owners cause them to behave irrationally as well. Because there is so much chatter about markets, the economy, interest rates, price behavior of stocks, etc., some investors believe it is important to listen to pundits – and, worse yet, important to consider acting upon their comments.
>
> Those people who can sit quietly for decades when they own a farm or apartment house too often become frenetic

when they are exposed to a stream of stock quotations and accompanying commentators delivering an implied message of "Don't just sit there, do something." For these investors, liquidity is transformed from the unqualified benefit it should be to a curse.

Mr. Buffett then went on to add,

If "investors" frenetically bought and sold farmland to each other, neither the yields nor prices of their crops would be increased. The only consequence of such behavior would be decreases in the overall earnings realized by the farm-owning population because of the substantial costs it would incur as it sought advice and switched properties.

Nevertheless, both individuals and institutions will constantly be urged to be active by those who profit from giving advice or effecting transactions. The resulting frictional costs can be huge and, for investors in aggregate, devoid of benefit. So ignore the chatter, keep your costs minimal, and invest in stocks as you would in a farm.

Mr. Buffett's analogy, clever as it is, still leaves unanswered how you decide whether or not to buy a farm. That is the question we turn to next.

FUNDAMENTAL VALUATION

Mr. Buffett's farm, like any business, creates value for its owner by providing the owner with cash that can be converted to consumption. With respect to stocks, they have value only to the extent that they produce cash payments for their owners. Unlike art or jewelry, stocks provide no non-pecuniary enjoyment. In fact, stock no longer even exists in paper form. Shares are simply entries in a computer. Therefore, estimation of the fundamental value of a stock requires an assessment of the future cash flows ownership of the stock will provide. This can be seen most clearly by taking the perspective of all investors as a group. As we noted earlier in the discussion of Sharpe's arithmetic, one investor may sell shares of Apple stock to another, but unless Apple buys the shares back, there is no way for investors as a group to rid themselves of the stock. From the perspective of the group, the stock has only one source of value – the cash payments that Apple makes to its shareholders.[3] Ultimately, therefore, the value of a share of stock must be determined by its pro rata portion of those disbursements. That is basic concept underlying valuation and fundamental security analysis.

FREE OR "DIVIDENDABLE" CASH FLOW

Because most cash disbursements to shareholders are in the form of dividends, it seems to follow that the value of a share should depend on expected future dividends and theoretically that is correct. The problem is that dividends are difficult to predict because they depend on the payout policy adopted by management. For example, Google generates a large amount of cash the company could use to pay dividends, but chooses to build up its cash hoard instead of paying it out. For this reason, valuation is typically based on "dividendable" or free cash flow. This is the amount of cash the company has left over in a given year after satisfying the cash needs necessary to fund its operations and new investments.

---

[3]If a company is sold, then the cash payments would include those made by the acquiring firm, but that is a relatively rare event that we do not analyze here. In principle the cash received from a buyout is no different than ordinary cash disbursements such as dividends.

An example is useful to illustrate why it is free cash flow per share that determines a share's fundamental value. Imagine that on the first day of the year a company opens a bank account to handle all company-related transactions. As the company operates throughout the year, every receipt is deposited in the account and all company payments, including all payments for new investments, are deducted from the account. The account is used for no other purpose. On the first day of the year the bank account is assumed to have a zero balance. In addition, an automatic overdraft provision is available in case withdrawals exceed deposits.

At the end of the first year of business, the balance in the account represents funds that shareholders could withdraw from the business and spend. (If the balance is negative, it represents the new funds that must be put into the account to cover the overdrafts of the business.) To continue the example, assume that at the end of the year the balance of the account is withdrawn and either paid as dividends or deposited in an investment fund so that the bank balance is reset to zero by the start of the second year. In that case, the balance at the end of the second year represents the spendable cash generated in year two. Proceeding in this fashion, it is clear that each year's ending balance represents funds that are available to be paid as dividends, in other words dividendable cash. Because it is assumed that value is ultimately derived from spendable cash, the value of a share of stock will be determined by its pro rata share of this sequence of year-end balances. These year-end balances are precisely the company's annual free cash flows to equity.

The typical way to use the dividendable free cash flow to value a company's stock is to do so on a firm-wide basis because financial statements are reported in that form. The price of an individual share can then be calculated by dividing the market capitalization by the number of shares outstanding. Although we leave the detailed mathematical modeling to textbooks on valuation, there is one simple model that is too important to ignore because it illustrates several fundament concepts – the constant growth model.

THE CONSTANT GROWTH MODEL

Recall from the chapter on fixed income that the value of a bond equals the present value of the coupon and principal payments discounted at the market interest rate. The same is true of stock valuation with a couple of twists. First, there is no fixed maturity. The dividendable cash flows continue into the indefinite future. Second, the dividendable cash flows are not fixed, or even known in advance. Therefore, what must be discounted are forecasts or expectations of future cash flows. Third, the discount rate is more complicated because it must reflect the risk of the free cash flow stream. Finally, we make the assumption that those expected free cash flows (FCF) grow at a constant rate, The resulting equation is

$$P = FCF_1/(1 + k) + FCF_1 * (1 + g)/(1 + k)^2$$
$$+ FCF_1 * (1 + g)^2/(1 + k)^3 \cdots \qquad (5.1)$$

In Eq. (5.1), P is the value of the equity, FCF_1 is next year's cash flow, g is the growth rate of cash flows, and k is the appropriate risk-adjusted discount rate. The dots following the last term indicate that the equation goes on forever. Despite the fact that the equation has an infinite number of terms, it can be solved to yield,

$$P = FCF_1/(k\text{-}g). \qquad (5.2)$$

Finally, Eq. (5.2) can be used to derive an expression for valuation ratios which are prices divided by a measure of cash flow, in this case free cash flow (FCF). Dividing both sides by FCF_1 gives,

$$P/FCF_1 = 1/(k\text{-}g). \qquad (5.3)$$

Admittedly, the constant growth model is a special case because most firms, particularly younger ones, have not settled down to steady state growth. Nonetheless, the constant growth still provides useful insight into the basic factors that determine value and valuation ratios. Looking at Eqs. (5.2) and (5.3), two key factors are obviously the expected future cash flow, FCF_1, and its rate of growth, g. The larger the expected future cash flow and the greater its growth rate, the higher the price and the greater the valuation ratio.

For cross-company comparisons, the valuation ratios are more meaningful than the price because they adjust for the scale of a company. Clearly, big companies tend to be worth more than small companies, but there is no reason to believe that they are worth more per dollar of cash flow that they generate. Although Eq. (5.3) is written in terms of free cash flow, earnings are often used instead. Technically, this is a mistake, but it does not make a big difference in most practical situations. In either case, it is the expected growth that is the prime determinant of the valuation ratio. As an example, Amazon currently has a P/E ratio of 288, whereas the ratio for Target is 12. The market obviously has different expectations for the earnings growth of the two companies.

The second factor that affects valuation ratios is the risk embedded in the discount rate, k. We know from the chapter on risk and return that expected returns, which are the discount rates that investors require, can be approximated by the sum of the 20-year Treasury bond rate and the product of the company's Beta and the equity risk premium (ERP). The only element of the three that changes from company to company is the Beta. The higher the Beta, the greater the company risk premium and the greater the discount rate. A higher discount rate, in turn, leads to a lower price and a lower valuation ratio.

Although we have derived these results by applying the constant growth model, they are more general than that. The two key drivers of valuation ratios remain growth and risk. In order to compare the relative importance of the two factors, it is necessary to forego the assumption of constant growth.

A MORE REALISTIC MODEL

Although the constant growth model is useful for illustrating key valuation concepts, it is not very realistic, at least for most companies. Particularly early in their lives, companies cannot be expected to grow at a constant rate.

The details regarding how to build more realistic discounted cash flow, or DCF, models are covered in a number of excellent texts on the subject and we do not address them here.[4] There are, however, several basic principles that must be understood to appreciate how the models work.

First, DCF valuations are divided into two stages. During the first stage, which typically lasts 5–10 years, a detailed financial model is constructed. The model is based on forecasts of all the necessary financial metrics, such as revenues, costs, capital expenditures, and depreciation. The ultimate output of the financial analysis is a series of free cash flows for each year in the explicit forecast period.

Second, after the stage of detailed forecasts, the company is assumed to reach a steady state in which growth is constant.

---

[4]Three current valuation books are: Aswath Damodaran (2012). *Investment Valuation*, 3rd edition. New York: Wiley; Shannon Pratt (2008). *Valuing a Business*, 5th edition. New York: McGraw-Hill; and Tim Koller, Marc Goedhart, and David Wessels (2017). *Valuation*, 6th edition. New York: Wiley. For a more advanced and theoretical treatment, the leading MBA text is: Robert W. Holthausen and Mark E. Zmijewski (2014). *Corporate Valuation*. New York: Cambridge University Press.

This steady state runs from the end of the forecast period out into the indefinite future. The value of the company in the steady state, often called the terminal value or continuing value, is computed using the constant growth model.

Third, an appropriate risk-adjusted discount rate is estimated. It is common to use the capital asset pricing model (CAPM) in this exercise, as described in the previous chapter.

Finally, the discounted value of the annual cash flows and the steady state value is calculated using Eq. (5.4) below. In Eq. (5.4), we have assumed a five-year initial forecast period, so as to limit the number of terms in the equation. That is why there are five explicit cash flow forecasts, FCF_1 through FCF_5. In practice, the forecast period should extend until it is reasonable to assume that the firm has reached steady state. For some companies, that could be 10 years or more. Added to the explicit cash flow forecast is the terminal value, TV_5. The terminal value is calculated using the constant growth model going forward from the end of the explicit forecast period. The explicit cash flow forecasts have a big impact on the terminal value because they determine FCF_5, which is the level at which constant growth starts.

$$P = FCF_1/(1 + k) + FCF_2/(1 + k)^2 + FCF_3/(1 + k)^3$$
$$+ FCF_4/(1 + k)^4 + FCF_5/(1 + k)^5 + TV_5/(1 + k)^5 \quad (5.4)$$

Although Eq. (5.4) looks complicated, it is easy to implement in a spreadsheet once the components have been estimated.

The key to the entire exercise, what separates a potential superior investor from the average, is the ability to estimate the annual cash flows during the first stage. The estimation procedures for the discount rate and a steady state value are relatively "cookbook" and are described in detail in all of the textbooks referenced in footnote five.

With respect to the annual cash flows, however, it is a painstaking, fact-intensive exercise that requires a detailed understanding of the business. There is no short-cut method for understanding a business. Furthermore, the skills necessary to understand one type of business, say a railroad, may well not be useful in understanding a biotechnology firm or a social media company.

To help investors do fundamental analysis, websites have sprung up that make DCF models available. One of the more sophisticated is finbox.io. You can visit the site, click on a company, and the software will build a DCF model. The problem with this approach is that all the hard work is hidden. For example, I asked the software to build a 10-year DCF model for Apple computer and it returned a value of $173. But what does that value assume about future iPhones, or Apple's entry into the media business, or Apple pay, or Apple services, or the Mac computer line and so forth? To value Apple more accurately than the market, it is necessary to understand the business well enough to answer all those questions. The software does not begin to do that and with good reason. It is an immense undertaking. The most complete and transparent DCF valuations online can be found in Prof. Damodaran's blog, "Musing on Markets." He provides complete spreadsheets with all the details for a wide variety of well-known companies.

To put the matter another way, if you develop a deep understanding of a business that allows you to make relatively accurate cash flow forecasts, your valuation of the business will never be too far off the mark. If you do not have that understanding, proper estimation of the discount rate and the terminal growth rate, and proper application of the equations, will not protect you from making serious mistakes.

Undoubtedly the most famous fundamental investor is Warren Buffett. Because Mr. Buffett has a personal fortune approaching

$100 billion derived from his investing activities, he is widely hailed as the world's best investor. It is not surprising, therefore, people often ask what his "secret" is. The DCF model provides an answer to that question.

WARREN BUFFETT'S "SECRET" TO INVESTING

The first thing to note about Mr. Buffett's secret to investing is that it is not really a secret. In his letters to shareholders over the years, Mr. Buffett has made it clear how he approaches investing. The key, he reiterates again and again, is "understanding the business." He says he will never invest in a business he does not understand. In terms of the discounted cash flow model, understanding the business means being able to forecast future cash flows more accurately than the market during the initial stage. There is no mystery as to how Mr. Buffett does this. He carefully studies the businesses in which he invests. He evaluates the competition and the barriers to entry. He assesses the impact of potential taxation and regulation and so on. All of this is detailed, painstaking work. One thing that makes Mr. Buffett unique is his ability to bring together all the disparate information required to produce a forecast of the company's future cash flow. Given the forecasts of future performance, the DCF value of the business can be calculated and compared to the market price. Companies that can be purchased for less than the fundamental value produced by the DCF analysis are attractive. Once Mr. Buffett has made up his mind that the investment is attractive and decides to "buy the farm," he has the ability to avoid being distracted by short-run variation in market prices. All this is easy to say in theory, but a daunting undertaking in practice, as the foregoing Apple example makes clear. In his 2013 letter to Berkshire shareholders, Mr. Buffett described it this way:

When Charlie and I buy stocks — which we think of as small portions of businesses — our analysis is very similar to that which we use in buying entire businesses. We first have to decide whether we can sensibly estimate an earnings range for five years out, or more. If the answer is yes, we will buy the stock (or business) if it sells at a reasonable price in relation to the bottom boundary of our estimate. If, however, we lack the ability to estimate future earnings — which is usually the case — we simply move on to other prospects. In the 54 years we have worked together, we have never foregone an attractive purchase because of the macro or political environment, or the views of other people. In fact, these subjects never come up when we make decisions.

It's vital, however, that we recognize the perimeter of our "circle of competence" and stay well inside of it. Even then, we will make some mistakes, both with stocks and businesses. But they will not be the disasters that occur, for example, when a long-rising market induces purchases that are based on anticipated price behavior and a desire to be where the action is.

Most investors, of course, have not made the study of business prospects a priority in their lives. If wise, they will conclude that they do not know enough about specific businesses to predict their future earning power. I have good news for these non-professionals: The typical investor doesn't need this skill. In aggregate, American business has done wonderfully over time and will continue to do so (though, most assuredly, in unpredictable fits and starts). In the 20th Century, the Dow Jones Industrials index advanced from 66 to 11,497, paying a rising stream of dividends to boot. The 21st Century will witness further gains, almost certain to be substantial. The goal of the non-professional should not be to pick winners – neither he nor his "helpers" can do that – but should rather be to own a cross-section of businesses that in aggregate are bound to do well. A low-cost S&P 500 index fund will achieve this goal.

In all of this, it is not that Mr. Buffett does anything different from other fundamental analysts. He just does the detailed work with great patience, care, and discipline, and with knowledge of his own limitations. Those looking to emulate him should look forward to decades of training and hard work, not a quick tip or insight. Perhaps that is why a lot more investors talk about emulating Mr. Buffett rather than actually trying to do it. And perhaps that is why Mr. Buffett recommends doing as he says, not doing as he does.

A DETAILED EXAMPLE: TESLA

At SMBP, we try to emulate Mr. Buffett and use DCF analysis to make investment decisions. One of the companies on which we have focused is Tesla. In 2014, one of the current authors (Prof. Cornell), in conjunction with Prof. Aswath Damodaran, published an article that attempted to explain the run-up in Tesla stock using a DCF model of Tesla with 10 years of initial cash flow forecasts. At the time the article was published, Tesla was trading at $253 per share. In light of the high capital costs and the competitive nature of the automobile industry, among other factors, even when making assumptions most favorable to Tesla, the highest values the DCF model produced were on the order of $100 per share. The article concluded that Tesla was overpriced.

In the years following publication of the article, the price of Tesla continued to rise. In August 2017, with Tesla's stock price at $350, Prof. Damodaran posted online an updated version of the DCF model. Taking account of the good news that had arrived since 2014, including the success of the Model S and Model X and the immense number of orders for the Model 3, Prof. Damodaran arrived at a DCF value of $192 per share. For those who want to see examples of detailed DCF models, Prof. Damodaran's blog posts on Tesla are a good place to start. They can be found at http://aswathdamodaran.blogspot.com/search?q=tesla. At SMBP, our DCF models, which are similar to those posted by Prof. Damodaran, were yielding slightly lower values, on the order of $175.

The models implied that both Prof. Damodaran and SMBP disagreed with the market. The next question is why? A simple answer would be that we were simply wrong. The market price represents the weighted average view of all people who are willing to buy or sell the stock: what makes us think our view is more accurate? That question is certainly one any investor who has concluded that the market is mispricing a security should ask.

In the case of Tesla, we valued the company as a car company. We built a detailed financial model that allowed for very rapid growth and for Tesla to maintain margins equal to those of Porsche, which were the best in the industry. But with all of that our DCF model never yielded a value north of $200. We concluded that the market had apparently believed that Tesla was something more than a car company. It was a "technology energy company" that was going to change the world and electric vehicles were just the start. While we were aware the Tesla owned Solar City, that business had even lower margins than automobiles and was also highly competitive. Our humble conclusion was that the market was simply wrong.

The foregoing also illustrates another important attribute of DCF models: they allow you to reverse engineer what the market thinks. Take Amazon, for example. In our discussion of the constant growth model, we noted that Amazon had a P/E ratio approaching 300 and concluded on that basis that the market expected rapid growth in Amazon's earnings. That conclusion is correct as far as it goes, but it is not very specific. A more complete approach is to build a DCF model for Amazon and then to explore the level of cash flow forecasts that are necessary to equate the model price with the market price. That is what SMBP did in the case of Tesla to reach the conclusion that the market was valuing Tesla as more than a car company.

Based on our DCF analysis, SMBP decided to take a position on Tesla stock, but the price was too high, not too low. What to do? There are two basic ways to taking advantage of overpricing. One is to sell the stock short. The other is to trade derivatives. A brief review of each is helpful because fundamental valuation analysis is as likely to uncover overvalued stocks as it is to uncover undervalued stocks.

Short Selling

Short sellers sell stock they do not own. They do that by borrowing the stock from other investors and selling it. At some future point, hopefully when the price has dropped, the short seller repurchases the stock and returns it to the lender.

For example, a short seller may borrow Tesla stock when it is selling at $350, and repurchase it when the price has fallen to $250. After returning the stock to the lender, the short seller keeps the $100 profit.

There are some complications to short selling. First, the stock may be hard to borrow. When stock is difficult to borrow, an additional borrowing fee is charged. Second, an investor who is short the stock must make any payments associated with stock ownership, such as dividends, to the lender. Third, the lender can call the stock at any time. If a new borrower cannot be found, the short seller will be forced to repurchase the stock at what may be an inopportune time. Fourth, potential losses on a short position are unlimited because there is no boundary on how high a stock price can rise. Finally, because stock prices tend to rise to provide investors with positive expected returns, short sellers will tend to lose money unless the market realizes the error of its ways in a reasonable amount of time. For all these reasons, short selling is not for the faint of heart, but for an investor who believes the stock is sufficiently overpriced, short selling can be attractive. As of this writing, SMBP maintains a short position in Tesla stock.

Call Options

There are hundreds of different types of derivative securities. Here we discuss only call options, which are probably the best known and most widely traded. A call option gives its owner the right to purchase a security at a set price for a given period of time. For this right, the buyer of a call option pays the seller, generally called the option writer, an amount determined by the price of the option in the market. This payment is referred to as the option premium. An example illustrates how this all works.

In August 2017, when Tesla was trading at $350, SMBP wrote (sold) call options on Tesla stock. The options give the buyer the right to buy Tesla shares at $350 any time prior to January 18, 2018. For that right, the option buyer paid SMBP, through the mechanism of the public option market, a premium of $38 per share.[5]

---

[5] The option price is often referred to as the option "premium," but that is just another word for price in this context. It has no relation to risk premiums.

Because call options give the option holder the choice whether or not to exercise, it can be shown that if the stock pays no dividend, like Tesla, it never pays to give up the choice by exercising the option before maturity. Therefore, the profit or loss from writing the options can be calculated as a function of the price of Tesla on the expiration date of January 18, 2018. If Tesla's price is below $350 on that day, SMBP keeps the $38 as profit. If the stock closes somewhere between $350 and $388, SMBP will have to use some of the $38 to buy back the options, but will still make a profit. The options will be worth the difference between the market price and the contract price. For instance, if Tesla is trading at $380 on January 18, the options will be worth $30. Above $388, SMBP has a loss that rises dollar for dollar with the stock price. If Tesla is trading at $450, the loss will be $62 dollars or 163% of the $38 received from writing the options. Thus writing naked options is a type of short selling, but the payoff is more complicated.[6] Exhibit 5.4 shows the option payoff at maturity. It illustrates that the profit is limited to the option price, but the possible loss is unbounded. However, there are offsetting benefits to the potential for large percentage losses. For one thing, writing options does not involve borrowing the stock, so all the costs of finding a lender and maintaining the short position are eliminated. In addition, profits can be earned by writing options even if the market never sees the error of its ways. For instance, the exhibit shows that if the stock price of Tesla remains parked at $350, the options will expire worthless and SMBP will collect the full option premium. The stock price does not actually have to drop as it does to allow profit from a short position. The fear, of course, is that the stock will become more overpriced and that the percentage losses will be large. That brings to mind the old Wall Street adage that "the

---

[6]Naked writing means selling options without owning the stock.

EXHIBIT 5.4 Tesla option payoff at maturity.

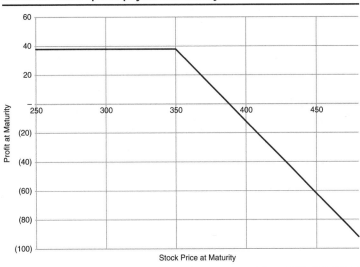

Stock Price at Maturity

market can remain irrational longer than you can remain solvent." The adage is a good tip for option writers to keep in mind.

HOW THE MARKET SETS STOCK PRICES

Fundamental valuation, in conjunction with an asset pricing model like the CAPM, forms the basis for the modern understanding of how the stock market sets prices. First, the fair risk-adjusted return is estimated by application of an asset pricing model. That risk-adjusted return sets the discount rate. Next, company free cash flows are projected and discounted to present value as shown in Eq. (5.4) to estimate the fundamental value. If the market price is less than the fundamental value, the theory predicts that investors will buy the stock. As they purchase the stock, the price rises until it reaches the fundamental value. If the stock is overpriced, investors shun or short the stock until the price has fallen to its fundamental value.

Though the mechanism makes perfect sense in theory, its actual operation in practice involves filling a lot of gaps. For example, we have pointed out that finance scholars, after more than 50 years of research, still cannot agree on the proper asset pricing model. Further, once an asset pricing model is picked, say the CAPM, the Betas are measured with a lot of error. This combination means that discount rates are estimated with a good deal of imprecision. Estimates of future free cash flows are likely to be even more imprecise. We have stressed how difficult it is to understand a business well enough to project its future performance with reasonable accuracy. The result is that the equilibrating mechanism is weak at best. It is for this reason that Lawrence Summers has consistently claimed that stock price can become disconnected from fundamental value for extended periods. It is this possibility, of course, that opens the door for sophisticated fundamental investors like Mr. Buffett to make superior risk-adjusted returns.

We find the following analogy to be helpful in thinking about the relationship between stock prices and fundamental values. Think of a water skier being attached to the boat not by a rope but by a bungee cord. The boat represents the fundamental value of the business and the skier represents the stock price. At the times, the skier lags behind the boat and the cord stretches. At other times the cord contracts and the skier comes flying past the boat. In the long run, however, there is a limit on how far the skier can stray from the boat.

The reason the skier and the boat do not move in tandem is because the fundamental value of the company is unknown. Depending on circumstance, including investor sentiment, estimates of that fundamental value change and that is what causes to cord to stretch and contract. But there is a limit on how far the skier can get from the boat. The market may not know the true fundamental value of Google, but it knows that it is more than the value of Groupon.

Aside from constructing personal valuation models, fundamental analysis can also be used to reverse engineer the market's expectations regarding a company's future cash flows. This reverse engineering is especially important in the case of transformative companies like Tesla, Netflix, Amazon, Google, and Facebook. It is easy to get caught up in the hype about all the wonderful things such companies are going to do and to lose track of the fact that the outlook for such companies is not lost on the market. The critical issue for making an investment decision is not whether or not a company's future looks bright, but whether or not it looks brighter to the investor than to the market. The only objective way to answer that question is to build a valuation model and see what cash flow projections are required to produce the current market price. If your projections are even more optimistic, then the stock is a potential purchase. But it is also possible that although your projections show rapid growth, the growth assumptions impounded in the current market price are even more optimistic. That was the case, for example, with SMBP and Tesla. The SMBP model projected rapid growth for Tesla, but not as rapid as the stock market price implied. Although SMBP agreed that Tesla was a transformative company, the stock was a sell.

FUNDAMENTAL INVESTING AND DIVERSIFICATION

There is a hidden cost (or one might say benefit) to fundamental investing, which is that it implies holding a poorly diversified portfolio. The active fundamental investor will typically be significantly over-weighted, relative to the market portfolio, in securities deemed to be underpriced and under-weighted or even short stocks deemed to be overpriced. Warren Buffett's holdings of publicly traded stock is a good example. Berkshire Hathaway owns publicly traded stock in less than 50 companies and more than half of the value is concentrated in less than 10 stocks. Such lack of diversification works great if you can identify mispriced securities, but if you fail, you bear added risk with no offsetting benefit. Furthermore, recall that Prof. Bessembinder found that only 4% of listed stocks accounted for virtually all the stock market value creation. An investor who held a limited number of stocks and happened to miss out on the 4% would do very poorly relative to a passive investor who held the market portfolio.

FINDING MISPRICED STOCKS

There is another problem that arises when attempting to pursue an active investment strategy using fundamental analysis. Which companies do you analyze? There are no flashing lights that say, "look at this stock." The fact of the matter is that in a competitive stock market most stocks are going to be fairly priced. If that is the case, and if an investor's DCF analysis is well done, the investor is likely to conclude that the stock is fairly priced. Consequently, an investor may have to analyze dozens of stocks before coming across one that appears to be mispriced. That analysis is time consuming and expensive. It is another cost of active as opposed to passive investing.

WHAT TO DO IF MISPRICING GETS "WORSE"

Suppose you have done your fundamental analysis and found a stock that you feel is underpriced. You buy the stock and its price falls, both in absolute terms and relative to the market. Assuming that your valuation model is unchanged, what do you do? There are two opposite choices and they depend on the confidence you have in your valuation model. If you have the patience and confidence in your position of a Warren Buffet, the appropriate response is to increase your position. If it was mispriced to begin with, it is mispriced to a greater extent now, warranting a larger position. On the other hand, the price drop is evidence that the market disagrees with you. That may cause you to reconsider your analysis and place more weight on the probability that you were wrong. If that is the case, the appropriate response is to reduce the size of the position. Finally, in light of the old adage that the market can remain irrational longer than you can remain solvent, if you truly believe in your position it should not be so large that you can be forced to liquidate it prematurely. These are all tricky issues that active investors face.

HOW DO YOU TELL IF THE MARKET IS "EXPENSIVE?"

So far, we have been focused on individual companies. However, fundamental analysis can also be used to analyze the level of stock prices generally. The level of an index like the S&P 500 does not convey information about whether the market is "high" or "low" because the index keeps growing over time along with the economy. Therefore, the fact that the index is higher now than it was 10 years ago does not tell you much about the relative valuation at either point in time. In this regard, valuation ratios are more useful. Although both prices and earnings expand over time, the ratio of the two is bounded because neither grows faster than the other in the long run.

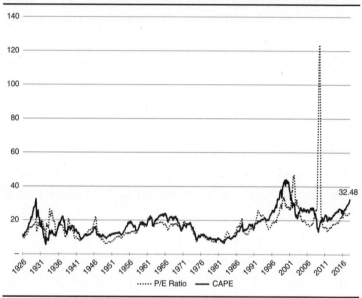

EXHIBIT 5.5 Last 12 months P/E and Shiller CAPE ratios: 1926–2017.

Exhibit 5.5 plots two measures of price to earnings for the S&P 500 over the period from 1926 to 2017. The first is the standard P/E ratio based on earnings over the last 12 months. The second is Nobel Prize winner Robert Shiller's cyclically adjusted P/E ratio (CAPE), which uses a 10-year average of past earnings instead of the most recent 12 months. A quick look at the exhibit makes it clear why Prof. Shiller prefers the CAPE ratio. If short-term earnings are depressed, but expected to recover, the standard P/E ratio will soar. This happened during the financial crisis. Although stock prices dropped, earnings collapsed to near zero. As a result of the denominator approaching zero, the P/E ratio for the S&P 500 jumped to more than 100 in 2009, a number way beyond its normal range. By averaging earnings over the last 10 years, the CAPE eliminates the impact of such anomalies and gives a more accurate picture of the relation between price and earnings.

Exhibit 5.5 shows that although the CAPE is trendless, it is far from constant. It ranges from below 10 in the early 1980s to above 40 in the dot.com boom of the late 1990s. It is worth noting that it has been above 30 only three times: in 1929, during the dot.com boom, and currently (November 2017). In the first two instances stock prices dropped sharply following the peaks of the CAPE. Does that mean the market it overpriced now? It depends on whether the CAPE should remain constant or whether its fair value can change. Here DCF analysis is helpful.

Although the constant growth model may not be applicable to individual stocks, it works well for the market as a whole. In the long run the aggregate value of stocks and the aggregate earnings must be tied to the growth rate of the national economy. If stock prices and earnings grew faster than the overall economy, eventually earnings would exceed the entire gross domestic product (GDP), which is impossible. Long before that, economic and political forces would constrain the rise of earnings relative to other components of GDP such as wages. This pattern can be seen in the past data. Exhibit 5.6 plots corporate profits as a percentage of GDP. While the line tends to rise during booms and fall during recessions, it is trendless. Thus the exhibit implies that in the long run, corporate profits and GDP must grow at the same average rate.

In light of the foregoing, it may be possible to explain the high current level of the CAPE ratio if economic growth is greater now than it has been in the past. Unfortunately, if anything, the reverse is true.

Exhibit 5.7 plots the rolling five-year average growth rate of GDP from the period following the Second World War until the present. The five-year average smooths the data and makes it easier to spot trends. If your eyes are good, you can probably see that the rate of growth has fallen in the last two decades. On this basis, the

EXHIBIT 5.6 Corporate profits as percentage of GDP: 1950–2016.

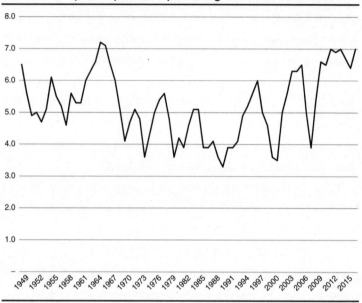

EXHIBIT 5.7 Rolling five-year average real GDP growth: 1954–2016.

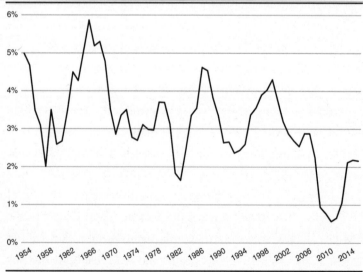

equilibrium CAPE should currently be lower that it was in the past, not higher.

Risk is a more promising possibility. In the chapter on risk and return, we argued that there was evidence that the ERP was falling. If that is so, the k in Eq. (5.3) will be declining and valuation ratios should rise.

Taking both growth and risk together, a fair conclusion is that any changes in the equilibrium CAPE ratio should be small. But if the CAPE ratio is trendless and tends to return to its mean value, can't that be used as a strategy for beating the market by buying when the CAPE ratio is low and selling when it is high? The short answer is not really. If such a strategy were an obvious method for making dramatically superior risk-adjusted returns, it would have already been exploited in a competitive market. Prof. Shiller began publicly posting the ratio decades ago, so it is no secret. But a straight "no" is too strong an answer. There is evidence that, on average and over the long run, the CAPE ratio has predictive power. Numerous academic and practitioner studies have shown that investors who buy the market index when the CAPE ratio is high tend to earn lower returns over the next 10 years than investors who buy when it is low. The statistical power of this conclusion is low, however, given the volatility of stock returns. The relation is only a tendency and by no means a sure thing. If you like the water skier example, the CAPE ratio can be thought of as the tension on the bungee cord. When the cord is slack (the CAPE ratio is high) increases in fundamental value place little upward pressure on stock prices because prices have already outrun the boat.

Finally, it is possible that a portion of the predictability of the CAPE ratio is to variation in the risk premium. In bad times, like the financial crisis, people are scared and require a large risk premium. As a result, stock prices fall and the CAPE ratio will be low, but expected future returns will be high to compensate people for bearing the perceived risk. On the other hand, during boom times when fears have receded, the CAPE ratio will be high and expected returns will be lower.

Despite the foregoing caveats, the CAPE ratio is worth tracking. When it is well above its historical average, investors should be more careful. The current situation is a prime example. The fact that the CAPE ratio is more than 30 is a flashing red light.[7] It will be interesting to see what the next 10 years bring in terms of average stock returns.

There is one other widely used stock market indicator, commonly referred to as the "Buffett indicator" because Warren Buffett has advocated its use. The indicator is the ratio of total stock market capitalization to GDP. The Buffet indicator is useful not only to assess the level of the market, but also to serve as a warning on the application of such indicators.

In Exhibit 5.8, the stock market capitalization to GDP ratio is plotted using Federal Reserve data over the period from year-end 1974 to year-end 2016. At first glance the Buffett indicator seems to say that the market is at an all-time high, but there is a caveat. Unlike the CAPE ratio the series is what statisticians call "nonstationary." The detailed definition of "stationarity," which is important when interpreting historical financial data, is postponed to Chapter 7, but for now it means that the Buffett indicator has a trend. This can be seen by using Excel to add a trend line, which is shown as the dotted line in the exhibit. Relative to the trend the current ratio does not appear to be out of line, but even that

---

[7]Of course, by the time this book is published readers will know whether the warning was warranted. At SMBP, we are reducing our exposure to the market because of the level of the CAPE ratio as of November 2017. Time will tell if this was a mistake.

EXHIBIT 5.8 Stock market cap/GDP: 1974–2016.

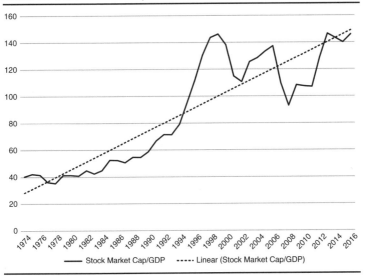

Stock Market Cap/GDP ----- Linear (Stock Market Cap/GDP)

is misleading. The Federal Reserve started reporting the ratio at the end of 1974, which coincided with the end of a vicious bear market. By year-end 2016 the market was in the seventh year of a strong bull run.[8] A trendline which runs from a low point to a high point will have overstated slope. There is another problem with the trend – namely that it cannot continue indefinitely. The valuation of the stock market is clearly tied to economic activity as measured by GDP. While the ratio can rise for a while, eventually forces will come into play to halt the increase. Exactly what those forces are and how they will impact the trendline is difficult to determine. The takeaway from all of this is that the Buffett indicator gives

---

[8] The words "bear market" and "bull market" need to be interpreted carefully. We use the term "bear market" to mean a period when prices were observed to have dropped, and vice-versa for a "bull market." These are ex-post concepts. Neither term should be interpreted as having predictive power. Too often people use the term bull market to mean that prices have risen *and can be expected to keep rising*. There is little basis to support such an expectation.

some support to the CAPE finding that the market was "expensive" at the end of 2017, but the conclusion is greatly influenced by how the trend in the indicator is calculated. This is a problem with virtually all market indicators. They need to be interpreted with great care.

THE SOCIAL BENEFITS OF FUNDAMENTAL INVESTMENT ANALYSIS

You might not think of fundamental investors trying to beat the market as people making an important social contribution like firemen or volunteer teachers, but you would be wrong. Even the most selfish, profit-oriented investors are performing a critical social function – deciding how to allocate scarce resources.

As the senior author of this book, I recall traveling in the Soviet Bloc countries in 1969. I discovered that I could purchase blue jeans in Paris or West Berlin and sell them for nearly 10 times the purchase price to desperate Russians. At the time, the amount and type of blue jeans produced in Russia was part of the Soviet five-year plans. Perhaps not surprisingly, the older Russian bureaucrats who were in charge of the five-year plans did not see the need for a socialist society to allocate significant resources to the production of blue jeans, let alone to their design and marketing. Because of the scarcity, owning a pair of fashion-forward Western jeans became a status symbol in cities like Warsaw, Prague, and Moscow and price of jeans skyrocketed.

The production of blue jeans may not seem like an issue of great social importance, but what about the production of steel? How much steel should the United States produce internally and to what extent should it rely on imports. That depends on how the market values domestic steel companies. Or consider the case of retailing. How much should be invested in online companies compared to brick and mortar firms? The soaring price of Amazon stock has attracted new capital to online firms.

The United States does not have five-year plans. To a large extent, the U.S. relies on the capital market to answer questions like those above. If producing electric cars seems like a good idea to investors, which means that investors calculate high DCF values for electric car companies, electric car companies will command high stock prices and attract capital. If selling cigarettes is seen as a declining business, cigarette company stock prices will fall and the firms will shrink. Of course, many people will not be happy with the market allocation. Some will say, for instance, that too much capital is allocated to hip-hop as compared to classical music. But that is because their values are at odds with the more common values reflected in market prices. The market allocates capital based on the way people actually behave, not the way they should behave.

For this system to allocate capital wisely, stock market prices must reflect the fair values of companies. And that is where fundamental investors come in. By studying businesses in detail, and estimating what their stock prices should be based on forecasts of future cash flow, fundamental investors drive prices toward that fair value. In doing so, these investors play a central role in the capital allocation process.

Notice that the social benefits provided by active fundamental investors may be a good deal greater than the private benefits they receive. Remember that Sharpe's arithmetic implies that active fundamental investors can do better than passive investors only to the extent that other active investors do worse. If the market is highly competitive and mispricing is rare, then it will be very hard for active fundamental investors to earn much in the way of superior returns. Society ends up being the main beneficiary of their attempts to beat the market.

CONCEPTUAL FOUNDATION 5

Conceptual foundation 5 is that the value of a security, including common stock, is derived from the future cash flows that the security produces. Recognizing this fact, fundamental analysis values securities based on forecasts of future cash flow. Investment decisions can then be made by comparing the estimated fundamental value of a security with the market price. While prices may diverge from fundamental value in the short run, the theory is that in the long run they will converge. And even if they do not converge, the fundamental investor is still protected because he or she receives the cash flows the security produces.

Investment decisions can also be made by attempting to predict when prices will rise without regard to fundamentals. In our view, this is more speculation than investment. It is an effort to discern whether someone will pay more tomorrow than the price today. Such efforts lie more in the realm of psychology than finance. Furthermore, efforts to guess what others will pay tomorrow can produce self-reinforcing bubbles that can lead to dramatic price increases and even more dramatic price declines.

6

TRANSACTION COSTS, FEES, AND TAXES

The ultimate value of an investment is determined by how much it contributes to your consumable wealth. That depends not only on how much the value of a security or portfolio increases, but also on what fraction of that increase you get to keep. There are three basic reasons why you keep less than 100%: transaction costs, fees, and taxes. We will take a look at each in turn, but before that it is helpful to get an idea of how important these factors might be.

Exhibit 6.1a plots the nominal path of wealth (POW) for the Center for Research in Securities Prices (CRSP) index, which we saw in Chapter 1. The three lines below the top line show what the POW would look like if transaction costs, fees, and taxes reduced the returns on the market index by 1 percentage point, 2 percentage points, and 3 percentage points. Exhibit 6.1b repeats the exercise using real returns.

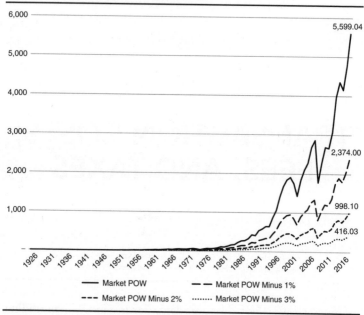

EXHIBIT 6.1a **The impact of cost on performance: nominal stock market POWs 1926–2017.**

The exhibits show that the long-run impact of the costs is dramatic. The reason is that unlike stock returns, which are highly volatile, costs are a consistent drag every year. While in any particular year costs may seem small relative to the market movement, particularly if the market movement is large, over the decades their impact cumulates and becomes a major determinant of performance. In the case of nominal returns, ending wealth drops from $5599 to $2374 to $998 to $416 as the costs rise from zero to 1 percentage point, 2 percentage points, and 3 percentage points, respectively. The picture is the same for real returns. Without costs the inflation adjusted end-of-period wealth is $406, but when costs are 3 percentage points it drops all the way to $30.

Given their importance, costs are clearly something an investor should not ignore. To complicate matters, the extent of the costs

EXHIBIT 6.1b **The impact of cost on performance: real stock market POWs 1926–2017.**

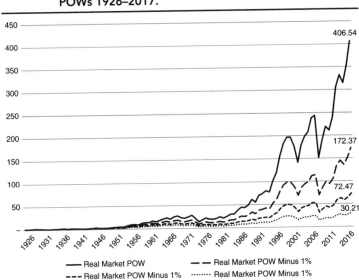

an investor pays is not always evident. For instance, when trading small stocks, the most important cost is not fees paid to the brokerage firm – those have been driven down by competition and technological innovations, but the impact of the bid-ask spread. That impact, however, depends on the specific stock being traded and the size of the trade, among other things.

Because they can have such a significant impact on long-run investment performance, it is worth examining some of the details related to each of the three major categories of costs: transaction costs, fees, and taxes.

TRANSACTION COSTS

By definition transaction costs are proportional to the amount of trading. The level of trading is generally measured by turnover. In the equity market, annual turnover equals the total value of

EXHIBIT 6.2 **United States stock market turnover in percent: 1975–2015.**

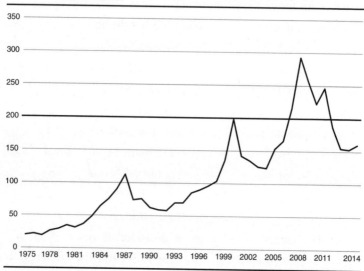

shares traded divided by the average market capitalization during the year. Exhibit 6.2 plots the turnover for U.S. stocks from 1975 to 2015. The exhibit shows that turnover has grown dramatically, rising eightfold from 20% in 1975 to 160% by 2015. Two factors have helped fuel this rise. First, technology has made it much easier to trade, and opened the door to algorithmic trading where computers constantly buy and sell in time periods of seconds or less. Second, improvements in technology have also helped promote a dramatic reduction in trading costs. That reduction, in turn, has been partially responsible for the rise in turnover.

The turnover rate provides insight into trading behavior. A turnover rate of 200%, which the market surpassed on several occasions, means that every six months the average investor sells his or her entire portfolio and replaces it with something new.

This clearly suggests that large swaths of the market are neither passive nor fundamental investors.

When you sell one stock to buy another the only thing that happens for sure is that you pay two transaction costs. If the market is efficient, so that all stocks are fairly priced, then you end up right where you started with a fairly priced stock, minus two transactions costs. The more actively you trade, the greater the drag on your investment performance due to transaction costs.

Trading involves two types of transaction costs: fees paid to exchanges and brokers and market bid-ask spreads. Competition among brokerage firms and exchanges has markedly reduced fees. For example, SMBP recently sold 10,000 shares of an S&P 500 Exchange Traded Fund (ETF) with a market value $2,436,000. The fees to the brokerage firm were $4.95 and the exchange fees were $56.27. The total fees of $61.22 amount to only 0.003% of the value of the trade.

Competition and technology have also reduced the size of bid-ask spreads for actively traded securities. For instance, at the time the SMBP trade was executed, the spread for the ETF was 243.61 bid to 243.63 ask, which comes to 0.008% of the ask price. If the brokerage firm were able to execute the trade somewhere between the bid and the ask, the effective spread would be even less. Not all spreads are as low as those for an actively traded ETF; the spread depends on things like the price of the security and the volume of trading. Nonetheless, for actively traded stocks the spreads are remarkably small. The average bid-ask spread as a percentage of ask price for S&P 500 stocks was 0.042% in December 2017. This low spread is both a blessing and a curse. A blessing because trading costs are so low. A curse in that it produces an incentive for what might be excessive trading. Just because active trading has become cheaper does not mean that it has become wise.

Not all stocks trade at such small spreads. For small firms, particularly small firms in financial distress, spreads are much larger. For example, Acusphere, a small and financially troubled company with a market capitalization less than $100 million, trades at a bid-ask spread of over 25%.

As we leave the sphere of actively traded stocks, spreads start to widen. With the exception of Treasury securities, which trade at spreads comparable to stocks, the spreads on bonds are higher and more difficult to discern. This is due in large part to the problem of heterogeneity. All shares issued by a company are identical. If you have seen one Tesla share you have seen them all. That is not true of Tesla bond issues. Each issue is unique. They differ by coupon and maturity and most importantly by seniority. The seniority determines where in the queue the holders of a specific bond will be if the company is forced into reorganization and thereby affects the credit risk. As a result of differing seniority, bonds issued by the same firm can have markedly different credit risk. In addition to, and perhaps because of, the heterogeneity, bonds trade in a less transparent and less active market. Many bonds go for weeks without trading, making it difficult to discern what the market price is. To protect themselves against the price uncertainty, dealers in these bonds quote a wide bid-ask spread.

Fortunately, there is little reason for investors to actively trade bonds. High-grade bonds, as we noted in Chapter 3, are basically alike in that they respond to one central factor – the level of interest rates. This means there is no reason for an investor to exchange one high-grade bond for another because both will behave similarly. In the case of low-grade bonds, the Milken analysis holds.

If an investor believes a low-grade bond is underpriced, he or she can simply buy it and hold it, thereby reaping the high coupons. There is no need to wait for the market to appreciate the mispricing so that the bond can be sold at a higher price. Finally, to the extent that an investor wants to trade a security based on his or her predictions regarding future corporate performance, the securities to trade are stocks, not bonds. Not only are the bid-ask spreads smaller for stocks, but stocks are more sensitive to changes in a company's financial performance. The bottom line is that bonds are securities to buy and hold, not to trade. This reduces the impact of their higher bid-ask spreads, because the costs can be amortized over the length of the holding period.

The other way to reduce the costs of holding bonds is to buy them through a low-cost fund. As we saw in Chapter 2, investors are increasingly holding securities through funds. The role of funds as financial intermediaries is so important that it is worth exploring in greater detail. We will use the example of investing in low-grade bonds, but the concepts apply to all similar assets.

To review, the problems with investing in low-grade bonds are that they are heterogeneous and illiquid. The high trading costs make it difficult to diversify. All of these problems can be solved by a fund. The basic idea is simple. The fund buys a large portfolio of low-grade bonds and then issues shares (or limited partnership interests) that entitle the shareholder to a certain stated fraction of the income earned by the fund after expenses and management fees. Investors get into and out of the fund by trading the shares either with the fund itself or on an exchange in the case of an ETF. Because the purchases and sales of shares by investors tend to offset each other, the fund does not have to transact very often in the underlying securities, thereby greatly reducing transaction costs. In the case of ETFs, there is no need to transact in the underlying securities at all because investors trade the fund shares with each other through the exchange.

The task performed by the fund is an example of financial intermediation. The fund transforms hundreds of illiquid low-grade bonds into highly liquid fund shares. There is nothing new about the process. It is basically what banks have done for centuries. They hold illiquid assets like loans and issue highly liquid deposits.

There is one other problem that banks and some funds also solve – evaluating the underlying securities. As part of the lending process, banks assess the credit worthiness of the borrower. Depositors, therefore, do not have to evaluate the quality of loans themselves.[1] Actively managed funds, including active stock funds, hedge funds, and private equity funds, which we discuss below, perform similar information-processing services. In this respect, they are different from passive funds, which simply match certain indexes. The information-processing service, however, does not come cheaply, as we describe below.

As an example of intermediation, the Vanguard High-Yield Corporate Fund holds positions in 524 low-grade bonds, but it has an expense ratio of only 0.23% per year. For individual investors interested in low-grade bonds, such a vehicle provides a liquid, low-cost, diversified way of taking a position. Vanguard does not try to determine whether the bonds it holds are properly priced. To the extent that an investor feels that certain low-grade bonds are mispriced, individual bond holdings can be added to what is largely a diversified, passive strategy.

Moving beyond bonds, spreads tend to widen further. We postpone our discussion of alternative assets including real estate

---

[1] The safety of deposits is ensured not only by a bank's analysis of the quality of the loans, but also by a host of regulations and by government deposit insurance. This makes banks somewhat unique.

until the chapter on alternative investment, but two points are worth making now. First, assets with large bid-ask spreads are not appropriate trading vehicles. The cost of a round-trip buy and sell can be as much as an entire year's return. Second, the best way to hold these assets is typically through funds. For instance, in the case of real estate there are real estate investment trusts that purchase large diversified portfolios of properties and then sell shares or partnership interests to investors. In general, as intermediation services have become more efficient with the rise of ETFs, holding fund shares has become the optimal way to hold most illiquid assets. As financial technology continues to improve, the role of funds as intermediaries is likely to become even more widespread. The question that remains is choosing between passive and actively managed funds.

MANAGED INVESTMENT FUNDS AND FEES

From a conceptual standpoint, managed funds work the same way as passive funds. The fund holds a portfolio of securities and issues shares (or partnership interests) against them. The difference is that managed funds add investment selection to the list of services provided. For that service, they charge fees and have expenses that are significantly greater than passive funds. This is in part due to the fact that managed funds, in an effort to beat the market, have higher turnover than passive funds.

Actively managed stock funds (primarily mutual funds, pension funds, and ETFs), hedge funds, and private equity funds differ primarily in the types of investments they hold and the fees they charge. Traditional stock fund managers hold primarily common stock. Many of the active stock fund managers follow strategies similar to those that we described in the chapter on fundamental investing, but there are a variety of approaches. For obvious reasons, the details of how a fund makes its investment decisions are proprietary. Fees and expenses at active mutual funds and pension funds average about 1% (100 basis points) per year, but they can be as low as 25 basis points and as high as 150 basis points. Because of Securities & Exchange Commission (SEC) regulations, mutual funds are required to disclose their holdings on a periodic basis.

The term hedge fund originally arose to describe managers who held short as well as long positions. Today it means funds that can hold just about anything. Hedge funds are typically set up as general/limited partnerships. In this structure, the general partner assumes responsibility for the operations of the fund, while limited partners can make investments into the partnership and are liable only for their paid-in amounts. In order to be excluded from SEC registration, hedge funds are generally constrained to have no more than 99 limited partners. This means that most hedge funds are not available to small investors. That limitation has been circumvented by so-called funds of funds, which are specialized funds that hold limited partnership interests in hedge funds and issue shares to final investors. The general partner's responsibility is to market and manage the fund, and to perform any functions necessary in the normal course of business, including hiring the fund managers and managing the administration of the fund's operations. Because of the exclusion from SEC regulations, hedge funds do not face the same disclosure requirements as mutual funds and many are quite secretive. In some cases, secrecy itself becomes a marketing tool. The idea is that if you have a secret sauce, as many hedge fund managers claim, you would never disclose it. However, this secrecy makes it more difficult to measure the risk and assess the performance of hedge funds.

The other feature of hedge funds is the size of their fees. While fee structures vary, one of the most common is 2/20 which refers to 2% of assets under management and 20% of profits. At that fee level, you can see why many hedge funds are secretive. To justify such high fees, a hedge fund must convince investors that it can sufficiently outperform the market on a pre-fee basis, so that investors can still beat the market after paying the fees.

Private equity funds are specialized investment companies that provide financial backing and make investments in the private equity of startup or operating companies. Like hedge funds, private equity companies are typically general/limited partnerships. In fact, private equity firms can be thought of as hedge funds that specialize in investing in private companies. Fees charged by private equity firms are also similar to those of hedge funds.

To boost potential returns for limited partners, hedge funds and private equity firms make significant use of borrowed money. As the result of this leverage, the returns of successful hedge funds and private equity firms can be spectacular – in either direction. One famous hedge fund, Long-Term Capital Management (LTCM), was noted for aggressive use of leverage. For every $1 of equity capital, LTCM borrowed nearly $100 to leverage its positions. Unfortunately when the market turned against LTCM that leverage proved to be its undoing and the firm went bankrupt. Despite the experience of firms like LTCM, when fund returns are spectacularly positive, investors clamor to invest despite the high fees. Compared to a potential 100% return, even the hedge fund fees look small. Academic research has found that the flow of funds occurs despite the fact that, as we noted in Chapter 2 and will revisit in the next chapter, short-run performance has virtually no predictive power for future performance.

The case of John Paulson provides a perfect example. Paulson was an obscure hedge fund manager prior to the onset of the financial crisis. He became famous by taking a very large and highly leveraged short position in mortgage-backed securities. With the onset of the crisis, Paulson's fund made profits in excess of $10 billion dollars and Mr. Paulson personally raked in profits exceeding $4 billion. Not surprisingly, Mr. Paulson became an investment sensation. He was even the subject of a popular book, *The Big Short*, which was made into a movie. In response to the massive past profits, investors poured money into Paulson's fund. Unfortunately, over the five years following the financial crisis, the return on Paulson's fund was approximately −65%. The story illustrates the risk of chasing the huge returns that successful hedge funds report. If those past returns are not predictive of future performance, all the investor gets out of the chase are the transactions costs of moving money and the opportunity to pay 2/20.

TAXES

With rates up to 50% for wealthy investors, taxes clearly affect after-tax investment performance. This makes tax strategy an important part of investing. However, the U.S. tax code currently runs to 73,954 pages, so a book on the conceptual foundations of investing can hardly do justice to the subject. There are, however, two basic tax issues that all investors should keep in mind: the distinction between income and capital gains, and the distinction between realized and unrealized gains and losses.

Income Versus Capital Gains

Income is generally taxed at higher rates than capital gains. This fact is not particularly relevant to investors who hold funds. For such investors, the breakdown between income (dividends) and capital gains will be determined by the stocks in the fund and how fund management trades them. Investors who hold stocks directly gain the ability to choose the ratio of stocks that pay dividends to those that do not, thus altering the ratio of income to capital gains. That can reduce taxes because income is taxed at a higher rate than capital gains.

Some investors may fear that holding only non-dividend-paying stocks will be a drag on total return, but that thinking is incorrect. Remember that the expected return on a stock depends on its risk, not on whether it pays a dividend or not. When stocks pay a dividend, the price drops by the amount of the dividend, so there is a direct substitution of income for capital gain without any impact on total return. However, a strategy of focusing on stocks that do or do not pay dividends does have a cost in terms of reduced diversification.

Interest income is taxed at income rates unless the bonds are issued by a tax-exempt entity. Like the corporate bond market, the tax-exempt bond market is highly heterogeneous. Bonds are issued by state and local governments, educational institutions, public works projects, and hundreds of other smaller tax-exempt entities. The ratings of tax-exempt bonds cover the waterfront from AAA to being on the verge of default. As we write this, the territory of Puerto Rico, for instance, has $72 billion in bonds outstanding, none of which are rated investment grade.

As was the case for taxable bonds, most tax-exempt bonds are illiquid and trade, if at all, at high bid-ask spreads. Consequently, the best way to hold the bonds is through a fund, for the reasons described previously. The Vanguard Long-Term Tax-Exempt Bond Fund currently holds 3,669 bonds and has an expense ratio of 0.09%.

The decision whether to hold taxable versus tax-exempt bonds depends upon a comparison of the investor's tax rate with the tax rate impounded in bond prices. For example, the yield on the Vanguard Long-Term Tax-Exempt Bond Fund is currently 2.11% compared to a yield of 4.06% on the Vanguard Long-Term Corporate Bond Fund. Based on these two yields, the break-even tax rate is 48%. Unless the investor's marginal tax rate is greater than 48%, a rate which few investors pay, the corporate bonds are currently a better choice.

There is a particularly nefarious interaction between taxes and inflation that arises because taxes are computed based on nominal dollars, not real dollars. A simple example using interest rates illustrates the problem. Consider two different inflationary environments. In the first, the real interest rate is 1% and inflation is 2% so that the nominal interest rate is 3.02%[2] – rates comparable to those today on high-grade bonds. In the second, the real interest rate is 1% and inflation is 5%, so that the nominal interest rate is 6.05%. The investor is assumed to pay taxes at a rate of 30% on *nominal* interest income. Assume that the investor is investing $100. At a 3.02% rate of interest the end-of-period nominal amount is $103.02 and the real amount is $101.00. However, the investor pays tax on the entire $3.02 of nominal income. At a 30% tax rate that comes to $0.906. The effective tax rate is 90.6% so that the investor's after-tax real return is less than 0.10%. A tiny real return, but at least it is positive. In the second scenario, the $100

---

[2]Not 3.00%, because of the compounding term.

investment grows to $106.50 in nominal terms but is still $101.00 in real terms. However, the investor's tax bill is now 30% of $6.05 or $1.815. After paying the taxes, the investor is left with $99.185 in real terms – less than the initial investment. The effective tax rate is an astonishing 181.5%!

Although the calculation is easiest to do for interest income, it holds across the board. Total nominal return is always a combination of the real return and inflation. Taxes are levied on the nominal returns. When inflation accelerates, and some day it probably will again, real after-tax returns can easily become significantly negative because the investor is paying tax on both the real return and the part of the nominal return that is compensation for inflation. One way to partially offset the impact of the rising inflation tax is to hold assets like non-dividend-paying common stock that offer return in the form of capital gains rather than income and then postpone recognition of the gain.

Realized Versus Unrealized Gains and Losses

Capital gains taxes are levied when a gain or loss is realized, not when it occurs. This makes it possible to benefit from what is called the tax timing option by realizing losses and deferring gains. An added benefit of the tax timing option comes from the fact that long-term gains are taxed at lower rates than short-term gains. Therefore, losses can be realized when they are short-term, while deferring gains until they reach the long-term status.

The tax timing option is more valuable for investors who hold individual securities rather than diversified funds. The holder of a diversified fund pays taxes on the net capital gains taken across all securities in the fund. An investor who holds individual securities can choose which ones to sell and when to sell them. It is even possible to sell a stock, realize the loss, and then repurchase it. However, if the repurchase occurs within 30 days of the sale, the loss is disallowed, so be sure to wait.

Although postponing capital gains can partially offset the impact of the inflation tax, it can lead to some nasty long-term surprises. Suppose that you buy a stock in an environment in which inflation is 5% and hold it for 20 years, earning a nominal return of 5%. Despite the fact that the real return is zero, every $100 invested in the stock would rise to $265.33 in nominal terms. If you then sell the stock and the tax rate is 30%, you would owe $49.60 in taxes on an investment whose real value was unchanged.

We have only scratched the surface on taxes. Taxes, like fees and transaction costs, are something over which an investor has some control, unlike the random variation in asset prices. Often there is excessive focus on asset prices because swings in prices are attention grabbing. Over the long run, however, taxes, transaction costs, and fees can be just as important.

CONCEPTUAL FOUNDATION 6

Conceptual foundation 6 states that although the random fluctuations in asset prices are beyond the control of investors, costs are not. Careful management of transaction costs, fees, and taxes is a sure way to improve investment performance. Elimination of costs on the order of 1% per year can have a significant impact on long-term wealth accumulation. Cost considerations also imply that the best way for investors to hold less liquid assets is through low-cost passive funds.

7

CAN HISTORY BE TRUSTED?

The financial media are constantly comparing current market behavior with historical periods. But what exactly can an investor learn from financial market history? That turns out to be a difficult question to answer and it depends on three key concepts: data mining, stationarity, and model specification. Although the concepts may not be familiar, there is some added good news here. All three, but particularly the first two, have applications to random events in other walks of life.

Remember that back in Chapter 1 we concluded that there cannot be any clearly demonstrable historical patterns in stock returns that can be exploited to beat the market. If there were, sophisticated investors armed with the latest computers and software would find them, exploit them, and thereby eliminate them. So if history is to provide some clues to the future performance of asset prices, those predictions cannot be simple, obvious ones. And that is where data mining, stationarity, and model specification enter the picture. Before historical data can be properly interpreted, the potential impact of all three must be considered. The best way to see why is to start with one of the most famous and controversial alleged patterns in historical stock market returns: the small firm effect.

In 1981, as part of his PhD dissertation, Rolf Banz discovered an interesting phenomenon. What he called "small stocks," that is the stocks of companies with small market capitalization, had produced outsized returns relative to the predictions of the capital asset pricing model (CAPM) over the period from 1926 to 1981. The results were so dramatic and controversial that Banz's finding launched dozens of follow-up studies. Nonetheless, to this day, a debate still swirls around the small firm effect. The focus of that debate is on how to interpret the results reported by Banz and those who followed. Four competing interpretations have been offered, of which three involve the concepts mentioned at the outset.

The first interpretation is that small firm effect is what it appears to be – a way to earn superior risk-adjusted returns by investing in stocks of small capitalization companies. Proponents of this interpretation propose that behavioral or institutional factors dissuade investors, including sophisticated institutions, from buying small stocks. The Banz study simply uncovered a property of markets that was always there. According to this interpretation, the small firm effect, like the law of gravitation, is an enduring feature of asset pricing.

The second interpretation is that the small firm effect is an artifact of inadequate risk measurement. Recall from the chapter on risk and return that a large body of academic research indicates that the CAPM is too limited – there are risk factors other than the market. It is possible that smaller firms are riskier than average when risk is measured properly. If that is so, there is no small firm effect, there is just the proper risk–return trade-off. This is the position taken by Eugene Fama and his colleague Kenneth French. In a widely cited academic paper, professors Fama and French develop an asset pricing model that includes size as a risk factor. Perhaps not surprisingly, that model predicts that there is no size anomaly that can be exploited to beat the market. The size premium is just a risk premium. According to this interpretation, Prof. Banz's original study, which used the CAPM, suffered from model misspecification. Had he used a proper model, he would never have claimed there was a small firm effect in the first place.

A third interpretation is that although the small firm effect characterized stock pricing during the period Prof. Banz studied, it is no longer true today. This is an example of non-stationarity. During the earlier period the average return on small stocks was higher than the market average, but something changed in the marketplace so that the effect disappeared.

Proponents of this view argue that once the small firm effect was discovered, forces arose to eliminate it. First, if small stocks were consistently underpriced relative to their risk as Banz's data seemed to imply, clever entrepreneurs would start investment firms designed to exploit the mispricing. In the case of the small firm effect, that is exactly what happened. Rex Sinquefield and David Booth, two students of Eugene Fama, started Dimensional Fund Advisers (DFA), in part to exploit the small firm effect. In the years since its founding, DFA became an immensely successful firm that now has hundreds of billions of dollars under management.[1] Although it was the largest such company, DFA was not the only firm to attempt to exploit the small firm effect. According to the

---

[1] In an example of what goes around comes around, David Booth made a $300 million dollar gift to the University of Chicago business school that now bears his name.

third interpretation, the increased demand for small company stocks by firms like DFA drove up their prices and, thereby, at least partially offset the small firm effect. Second, if small firms had a higher cost of equity capital (remember the cost of capital for a company is the expected return for investors), then value could be created out of thin air by combining small firms. Put two small firms together, simply by forming a conglomerate without changing any of their operations, and you get a bigger firm by definition. You might think the bigger firm would be worth the sum of its parts because the combination did not change either of the underlying businesses, but that is not correct if the small firm effect holds. Because the combined firm is bigger, the small firm effect says that the cost of equity capital (the discount rate) is less. This reduction in the discount rate produces an added boost in value causing the combined firm to be worth more than the sum of the parts. Continuing in this fashion, value can be continually created by rolling up small firms into a big conglomerate. That process, however, would increase the demand for and drive up the price of small firms, ameliorating the small firm effect.

Adherents of this third interpretation claim that because of the offsetting activity it caused, the small firm effect has become an historic relic. You would think that this would be an easy claim to test. Prof. Banz's work was published in 1981 and was limited to U.S. data. Therefore, by using more recent data and data from other countries, it would be possible for researchers to determine whether the small firm effect has endured. Unfortunately, the newer and international data are ambiguous. Most recent studies show that the small firm effect, if it exists at all, is smaller than that documented by Prof. Banz. Whether or not the effect has disappeared entirely remains a subject of dispute.

The fourth interpretation is that there was never a small firm effect in the first place. Even a series of random numbers will have apparent oddities. If enough researchers all look at the same historical data set they will find oddities that are due to random fluctuations and that have no economic meaning. They are simply an artifact of data mining. The small firm effect, according to this interpretation, is just one example.

Notice that the fourth interpretation, like the third one, implies that the small firm effect should not be found in more current data. According to the third interpretation, based on non-stationarity, there should be no current evidence of the small firm effect because the world has changed. According to the data mining interpretation, there should be no current evidence of the small firm effect because there never really was one in the first place.

Before considering each of the three issues of data mining, stationarity, and model specification in turn, there is one more thing regarding the small firm effect that is worth noting. In Chapter 6, we pointed out that bid-ask spreads are much larger for small, particularly very small, market capitalization stocks. This makes it difficult to calculate the actual profitability of trading small stocks. The profits that appear on paper may not be achieved in practice. DFA has developed sophisticated trading procedures to reduce the cost of trading small stocks. However, those procedures require DFA's size and market connections. They would not be available to the average investor. So even if there is a vestige of the small firm effect, its exploitation may be limited to firms like DFA.

Putting aside concerns about the costs of trading small stocks, we now consider each of the three issues that make interpreting historical financial data so difficult.

DATA MINING

Randomness is a slippery concept. Often people think of a random data set as one that has no patterns. For instance, they would conclude that a random list of random digits would not have runs in which one integer is repeated. That is not the case. Ironically, the failure of people to appreciate this property of random numbers has been used to look for corruption in government. In order to hide corrupt activities, government officials sometimes have to forge economic data. To avoid making it appear that the books have been cooked, the corrupt officials often need to use random numbers. Those most familiar with statistics are wise enough to use a random number generator, but others simply write down what they think are a random sequence of digits. When they do so, they frequently fail to include enough patterns, such as runs of consecutive digits in the forged data. Their failure to understand randomness leads to their downfall.

A great example of a pattern in random numbers is the expansion of Pi. As a young man, the famous physicist and bon vivant Richard Feynman would reel off the first 768 digits of the expansion, the last six of which are 9-9-9-9-9-9, and then say "and so on" before breaking into laughter. His joke became so well known that the 763rd digit of Pi has become known as the Feynman point. Of course, Pi has been expanded to trillions of digits without any pattern being detected. Like any random series, the expansion of Pi has instances of apparent patterns. Without those patterns, it would not be random!

There is one more Feynman story that shows how history can trick people into finding meaning in random events. As an undergraduate studying in his room, Feynman had an intense premonition that his grandmother had died. At that very moment another student shouted, "Feynman you have a phone call." (The residence hall at MIT had only one phone back then.) Feynman headed toward the phone dreading what he was about to hear only to learn the call was from another student saying that he had left his book in the classroom. Feynman thought to himself, people must have premonitions like this all the time. Most of the time a premonition passes and nothing happens, so it is forgotten. But in a few rare cases, solely by chance, the premonitions are fulfilled. For instance, what if the call had been to say his grandmother had died? To many people, such as experience could be transformative – something they would never forget and often repeat. To Feynman, fulfilled premonitions were a perfect example of data mining. With enough people having enough premonitions, there were certain to be some remarkable coincidences. The same is true of financial markets. With enough researchers performing enough studies, they are almost certain to find a variety of apparent market anomalies.

The best way to check for data mining is to repeat an experiment. This is commonly done, for example, in the testing of new drugs. If the effect in question reoccurs in several independent trials, it is unlikely to be an artifact of data mining. Unfortunately, in the case of financial market history, we only get to watch the movie once. There is only one historical record of security price behavior. The fact that we now have evidence on thousands of stocks for almost a century in the United States is a two-edged sword. The large sample increases the power of statistical tests that can be performed, but it also increases the number of anomalies that will be uncovered by extensive data mining. What is needed is a new data set.

The best solution is to wait another century for nature to provide a new data set. That option, however, is not appealing to current investors. A more feasible alternative is to use heretofore unexamined international data. Although sample periods are shorter, there are fewer subject companies, and the data are usually not as clean, international data can provide an independent test of hypotheses. The problem is that with the explosion of global financial databases, unexamined data is becoming scarce.

Another alternative, proposed by Prof. Campbell Harvey, is to use a higher cut-off for determining what is a true investment anomaly rather than a random fluctuation. The standard statistical tests for an anomaly assume that the study under consideration is the only relevant one. But if there are hundreds of researchers and investors doing thousands of studies that criterion is clearly violated. The problem is that even a higher standard does not solve the problem entirely. Some data mined results will still get over the hurdle and those that do will attract inordinate attention.

NON-STATIONARITY

Let's get the mathematical jargon out of the way upfront. Formally, a stationary stochastic process is a stochastic process whose joint probability distribution does not change when shifted in time. Consequently, parameters such as mean and variance, if they are relevant, also do not change over time. Non-stationarity should not be confused with unpredictability. All random processes are unpredictable. If the process is non-stationary, even the parameters of the random distribution cannot be estimated with confidence.

Admittedly the formal definition does not mean much to those who have not studied statistics and it could be dispensed with if non-stationarity were not such an important issue. Fortunately, there is a more intuitive way to describe stationarity.

Consider a jug containing red, white, and blue balls. The jug is shaken up, a ball is drawn at random, and its color noted. Then the ball is put back in the jug and the process is repeated. Though it is unknown at any step what color ball will be drawn, the probability of drawing a red, white, or blue ball remains unchanged. There is no distinction between the first draw and the tenth draw or twentieth draw. Each replication of the experiment is effectively identical. That is what is meant by a stationary process.

It turns out that the sequence of digits in Pi discussed above is, as far as we know, a stationary process. It cannot be distinguished from a process of putting balls number 1 through 9 in a jug and repeatedly drawing a ball with replacement. The sequence of drawn digits is random, but the process by which the digits are selected is unchanging.

Now, suppose that in the middle of the experiment a second jug is suddenly introduced with a different combination of balls. If the next draw is from this second jug, the probabilities that applied to the first jug are no longer accurate. The nature of the random process has changed. It is no longer stationary.

If there are only two jugs, there is what can be called a limited degree of non-stationarity. By simply redefining the procedure for drawing balls, a new stationary process emerges that involves two steps. At the first step, one of the two jugs is randomly selected. At the second step, a ball is drawn from the chosen jug. As long as this procedure is followed the new process, though more complicated, is stationary. In some situations it may be possible to discern this type of more complicated stationary process.

The balls and jugs analogy is useful for conceptualizing differing degrees of non-stationarity. The important questions include: How many jugs are there? How is the jug from which the ball is to be drawn selected? What is the distribution of balls within each of the jugs? In the limit, think of the case where there are an immense number of jugs, the contents of which are unknown, and where the probabilities of selecting a given jug are also unknown and may be changing over time. This limiting case we refer to as fundamental non-stationarity. Although this may seem like an extreme case, we argue that it is a problem that investors face on a daily basis. When it comes to investing, fundamental non-stationarity is not a rarity, but the normal state of affairs. If that is so, what we can learn from market history is limited.

Non-Stationarity and the Small Firm Effect

Perhaps the most important parameter for the random process that describes stock returns is its mean value. If the mean is changing, the process is non-stationary. That implies that past averages *cannot* be used to predict reliably future expected returns. The third interpretation of the small firm effect makes the argument that the mean is changing. Early on, when Prof. Banz did his study, the mean had a higher value. After discovery of the effect brought arbitrage into play in the form of companies like DFA and roll-ups, the mean declined. As a result, historical results such as those reported by Prof. Banz could not be relied upon as a predictor of future average returns for small stocks.

Non-stationarity is far more pervasive than the small firm effect. It is likely to affect every aspect of financial markets. Consider for instance the case of Germany. Germany began the twentieth century as a monarchy and one of the richest countries in the world. It suffered a disastrous defeat in the First World War. In the years following the war, the Weimar Republic collapsed under the weight of lofty war reparations, depression, and soaring inflation, which led to the rise of Hitler and the Nazis. That led to another disastrous war and the division of the country. Following reunification in 1990, Germany went on to become a stable democracy with the most powerful economy in Europe. The thought that the random processes driving the returns on financial assets would be unaffected by such momentous social changes is clearly nonsensical.

Although Germany may be an extreme example, countries around the world are constantly experiencing social, political, and economic changes that are almost certain to affect the behavior of financial markets. That is why we believe that securities prices are fundamentally non-stationary. If we are correct, any attempt to project the past behavior of market prices into the future must proceed with great caution and skepticism.

What is true at the level of countries is also true at a more micro level. With regard to individual stocks, language is an impediment to appreciating the full extent of potential non-stationarity. For instance, throughout its corporate life Apple has always been called Apple, but the company has reinvented itself numerous times.[2] In the last three decades, Apple transformed itself from a start-up maker of personal computers into a global consumer product and services powerhouse, despite having several brushes with insolvency along the way. While it is conceivable that the process for stock returns remained stationary while the company was continually transformed, it would be foolhardy for an investor to assume that the dramatic evolution of the company had no impact on the expected return and the expected risk of Apple's stock.

---

[2]To be fair, the original name of the company was Apple Computer, which was shortened to Apple as other devices (which are actually computers) became the predominant source of the company's revenue. However, throughout its life the company has generally been referred to as Apple.

MODEL SPECIFICATION

We stated at the outset of the book that "beating the market" is defined as earning risk-adjusted returns greater than those on the market portfolio. As a result, deciding whether investment performance is superior depends on the model used for measuring risk. The second interpretation of Prof. Banz's results is that they are an artifact of using an inappropriate model, namely the CAPM, to measure risk. When more appropriate models are employed, such as the Fama–French three-factor model, the risk-adjusted returns on small stocks are seen to be in line with the market because their risk is greater than the CAPM implies.

There is nothing special about the small firm effect with regard to the issue of model specification. Investors and academic researchers are constantly searching for "anomalies" in asset prices that can be used to beat the market. Suggestions for such anomalies include: the low-variance effect, the value effect, betting against beta, the January effect, and the list goes on. In the case of each of these anomalies, there is a dispute about model specification. Remember that academic researchers claim to have found 316 different risk factors. Depending on which of those risk factors is chosen to include in a model, an effect, say the low-variance effect, can be interpreted either as a market-beating anomaly or as a risk premium. To date, this is an issue that remains largely unresolved for many alleged anomalies.

INTERACTION

In the case of the small firm effect, we treated the three issues – data mining, non-stationarity and model misspecification – as if they were separate issues. In fact, these issues will typically interact. It is likely that data mining was one reason that Banz found such a strong small firm effect in his original study. It is also likely that non-stationarity played a role as arbitrage came into play. Finally, the small firm effect may have been overstated because the CAPM did not provide the proper benchmark. It is the interaction of all three issues that makes historical financial data so devilishly difficult to interpret.

SMART BETA AND FACTOR PREMIUMS

We noted above that if size were related to risk, the size effect may be a risk premium. Even if it is, there may be investors who are willing to bear the risk of investing in small company stocks in order to harvest the risk premium. In this respect, size is not alone. Each of the hundreds of potential risk factors has its own potential risk premium. The strategy of trying to harvest those premiums has come to be called "smart beta" because there is a beta associated with each of the risk factors. Smart beta investing has become popular among institutional investors who are attempting to improve performance by harvesting the risk premiums. To decide which risk premiums to exploit, the investors calculate their historical averages. This raises a question regarding whether estimates of historical premiums are reasonable forecasts of future premiums. Remember that researchers went on a decades-long search for risk factors. That suggests that data mining could be a serious problem. It is also unclear whether the factors that were discovered are enduring as opposed to a transitory characteristic of a past period. In other words, non-stationarity may be an issue. For instance, research by Arnott, Beck, Kalesnick, and West suggests that the factor premiums are not true risk premiums, but are instead artifacts of the prices of stocks related to those factors rising. As we write this, the entire issue is unsettled. Further evidence of how difficult historical financial data are to interpret.

ASSESSING INVESTMENT MANAGEMENT PERFORMANCE

Perhaps the most common use of historical data is assessing the performance of active money managers. One thing that few investors appreciate is that even when superior performance exists, it may be difficult to identify because of the random fluctuations in asset prices. As an example, consider a simple thought experiment. An investor is presented with two coins. One is fair and has a 50% chance of landing heads. The other is biased and has a 60% chance of landing heads. The investor is given one of the coins. How many times must the coin be flipped for the investor to be 95% confident which one it is? When asked this question, typical answers are in a range of 10–50 flips. The actual answer is 143 flips.

Virtually all final asset holders, from mutual funds, to pension funds, to sovereign wealth funds, hire professional managers to make investment decisions for them. As a result, they have to decide how to evaluate and when to hire or fire managers. Academic research reveals that in making those decisions, institutional investors focus on recent performance relative to a selected benchmark. For example, the mandated benchmark for most professional managers running US large-cap equities is the S&P 500 index; managers would be considered to have outperformed if they produced excess returns against the S&P 500 over the evaluation period. That evaluation period is typically three years. Those managers who did particularly poorly relative to the benchmark are fired and replaced by managers who did particularly well. Notice that in light of the coin flip example this is a very short horizon. It is difficult to draw conclusions with a high level of confidence based on 36 months of performance.

Putting the small sample size issue aside, there are two fundamental reasons why one manager may perform better than another in a given three-year period. The first is what can be called skill. For instance, Tiger Woods is a skillful golfer (even after all his injuries). If a typical country club member competes against Tiger for 18 holes, the result will be the same virtually every time. In the same way, it is possible that one manager may be more skillful than another and outperform a majority of the time. The second is a variant of luck. Different managers employ different strategies. One may focus on technology companies, while another buys primarily value stocks. If in a particular period, say 2017, technology stocks do especially well, then the first manager will appear to be a superior performer. But that is only because his or her strategy worked well due to happenstance, not because that manager possessed and special skill.

One way to test whether the manager-selection technique used by institutional investors is effective is to compare the performance of managers who were hired to those who were fired during the subsequent three years. If the successful managers are more skillful, that skill should be evidenced in the subsequent period. If, however, their success is due to chance, they are not more likely than any other manager to outperform in the subsequent period. In a comprehensive study, Cornell, Hsu, and Nanigian found something interesting. The managers who were fired subsequently performed *better* than those that were hired. The difference was not large, but averaged across hundreds of managers over more than 20 years, the result was statistically significant. How could that be? Even in an efficient market, past winners should not underperform.

The answer is that there is evidence that stock prices are mean reverting. Mean reversion means that stocks that have run-up sharply in the past tend to perform a little more poorly in the future than those that have dropped and vice versa. The effect is not large, but it can be discerned when large data sets are analyzed. This mean reversion explains the results found by Cornell, Hsu, and Nanigian. The managers who were fired held stocks that had performed poorly during the evaluation period and, due to mean reversion, tended to do slightly better in the subsequent period. The reverse was true for managers who held stocks that had performed well. The irony is that to the extent that history tells you anything about past superior performers, it tells you to avoid them. It is dramatic evidence of the risk associated with misinterpreting the implications of historical financial data.

PRESIDENTIAL POLITICS AND THE STOCK MARKET

We close this chapter with one final example – the relation between presidential politics and the stock market. The example is typical of the type of results that are frequently reported in the financial press. It turns out that average excess stock market returns are much higher under Democratic than Republican administrations. A detailed study by Pastor and Veronesi reports that from 1925 to 2015 the average excess return under Democratic presidents was 10.7% per year compared to −0.2% per year under Republican presidents. The difference, almost 11.0% per year, is highly significant both economically and statistically. This raises an obvious question. Is there something about Democratic administrations that is highly beneficial for the stock market or is the result due to data mining?

This is a perfect hypothesis to test using international data. There is no reason to believe that the United States is unique with respect to the relation between stock prices and politics. If markets do better when the left-leaning party is in power compared to the right-leaning party, it should be observable in other countries. Following up on this idea, Arnott, Cornell, and Kalesnik studied whether there was a relation between the party in power and stock market returns in Australia, Canada, Germany, France, and the United Kingdom. The countries were chosen because they have developed stock markets and because each has experienced changes in political control over the last several decades between left-leaning and right-leaning parties. The authors found that outside of the United States there was no systematic relation between the party in power and stock market returns. In fact, the results showed that international stock markets did slightly better when the right-leaning party was in power but the results were not statistically significant.

Given the international findings, Arnott, Cornell, and Kalesnik went back to take a closer look at the U.S. data. They found that two key events were responsible for much of the differential returns under Democratic and Republican presidents. Specifically, a Republican was president during the two great financial and economic crashes, which began in 1929 and 2008, and, unsurprisingly, a Democrat was president during the subsequent recoveries. Had the order of the incumbencies been reversed, the effect would have been reversed. This supports the interpretation that the U.S. results are due to a combination of serendipity and data mining.

The example underscores the importance of not taking apparent patterns in historical financial data, even patterns that are economically and statistically significant, at face value. The problems of data mining, non-stationarity, and bad models are so important that results that appear too good to be true may, in fact, be too good to be true.

CONCEPTUAL FOUNDATION 7

When Hegel said that "We learn from history that we do not learn from history," he may have had investing in mind. Conceptual foundation 7 is that the implications of historical financial data for future financial performance are complex and nuanced. Data mining, non-stationarity, and model misspecification all make it difficult to conclude that a strategy that beat the market in the past will continue to do so in the future.

8

CAN BEHAVIORAL ANOMALIES BE EXPLOITED?

Let's start by reviewing what the standard "rational" finance model is before diving into what behavioral finance says is wrong with it. Recall that investors are assumed to maximize the utility associated with consumable wealth. That utility always increases as wealth rises, but at a decreasing rate. The fact that each added dollar provides a little less utility than the last is the basis for risk aversion. It is this risk aversion that drives rational asset pricing models. Furthermore, investors are assumed to be rational in their efforts to maximize utility. They do not succumb to fear and greed.

Taken at face value, the traditional model appears to most people to be clearly false. Can you think of anyone who is not affected by fear when the stock market is crashing? The field of behavioral finance, which has grown dramatically in the past two decades, has taken up the task of attempting to develop models of behavior that are, in their view, more realistic than the assumption of rational utility maximization. This effort has not gone unnoticed. Nobel prizes in economics have been awarded to Herbert Simon, Daniel Kahneman, and Richard Thaler, leaders in the growing area of behavioral finance, for providing evidence contrary to the assumption of rationality. But the fact that individuals evidence departures from rationality does not mean that those departures can serve as a basis for beating the market. After all, Richard Thaler is not a billionaire. From an investment standpoint, the ultimate question is not whether people routinely behave in ways that diverge from rational utility maximization, but whether those divergences from rational behavior lead to market anomalies that can be identified and exploited to earn superior returns.

But we are getting ahead of ourselves. The first step is to outline some of the contributions of behavioral finance. In this effort, a quote by Tolstoy comes to mind. In Anna Karenina, Tolstoy said, "All happy families are alike; every unhappy family is unhappy in its own way." In the traditional model, all investors are alike. They are all rational utility maximizers. In behavioral finance, investors exhibit all sorts of irrationality and each investor is potentially irrational in his or her own way. We begin, therefore, with a short taxonomy of the some of the main departures from rational utility maximization suggested by behaviorists.

A TAXONOMY OF POTENTIAL INVESTOR BIASES

Behaviorists often divide the errors and biases that cause behavior to diverge from rational utility maximization into two categories: cognitive errors and emotional biases. Cognitive errors are associated with Herbert Simon's notion of bounded rationality.

Because people have intellectual, informational, and conceptual limitations, they rely on heuristics and rules of thumb that often differ from proper statistical or mathematical analysis. Emotional biases arise as a result of attitudes, feelings, and predispositions that are at odds with rational calculation of the utility of consumable wealth. We consider each category in turn. Our lists are not meant to be exhaustive. We focus on the errors and biases most frequently analyzed in research papers. We also offer several examples of how the errors or biases may affect investment behavior.

COGNITIVE ERRORS

Conservatism Bias and Underreaction

According to behavioral finance, making an investment decision involves time commitment and mental energy. Experiments show that after making a decision people become invested in their initial views. By clinging to their initial viewpoint, they inadequately incorporate new information that is inconsistent with their decision. This is called conservatism bias. Investors exhibiting conservatism bias may underreact to new information causing them to hold a position longer than a rational investor would. For example, an investor who buys a stock may pay insufficient attention to new negative information.

Confirmation Bias

Studies in psychology show that people tend to notice and are more receptive to information that confirms previously held beliefs. One theory is that this is due to confirmatory information being easier to process cognitively compared to contradictory information. As a result, according to behavioral finance theory, individuals may give undue weight to evidence that conforms to their beliefs and ignore or modify evidence that does not. It has been suggested that confirmation bias leads to building large positions in a limited number of securities rather than diversifying.

Representativeness Bias

Like confirmation bias, representativeness bias is a belief perseverance bias. The hypothesis is that people have a tendency to use their past experiences and thoughts as a frame of reference to classify information into categories. When presented with new information they often use a "best fit" approximation to fit the new information into a category. This approximation can simplify and speed up human information processing. However, new information may not necessarily fit into the personalized categories in the real world, and therefore can be incorporated incorrectly. According to behavioral finance, representativeness bias can cause investors to avoid the energy and time necessary to process complex data and instead to rely on simple classifications. Those simple classifications can lead to poor portfolio allocation.

Hindsight Bias

It has been established in psychology that human memory does not present an accurate record of the past. Instead people tend to "fill in the gaps" of the past with what they prefer to believe. One aspect of this is that when looking back at an event, or investment decision, it is seen as being more predictable than it actually was at the time. For instance, after the tech crash in 2001, many investors claimed to have known that tech stocks were overvalued. As a consequence, investors can develop a false sense of confidence and underestimate investment risk.

Anchoring and Adjustment Bias

Anchoring and adjustment bias is an information-processing bias resulting from the manner in which the human brain estimates probabilities. The theory is that in dealing with probabilities the human brain is not like a computer. Instead, people often use heuristics, or rules of thumb, to generate estimates of the likelihood of outcomes. The theory says that this process begins with a starting point or "anchor." An example is the price at which an investor purchases a security. To a purely rational investor, there should be nothing unique about the anchor. However, according to this theory, people often give special weight to these "anchors." Similar to conservatism bias, this can cause investors to under-weight, and not to properly adjust to new information because of the undue emphasis on the anchor.

Framing Bias

To illustrate framing bias, imagine you are considering taking a new job, and one potential employer states "30% of new hires receive raises in their first year of employment," whereas a second potential employer says, "70% percent of new hires will not see any raises in their first year of employment." Though the two statements are mathematically equivalent, framing bias theory says that people often respond differently. If this is true, investment decisions could depend on the manner in which investment information is framed.

EMOTIONAL BIASES

Loss Aversion Bias

In their early work, Kahneman and Tversky in 1979 found evidence that people strongly prefer to avoid losses as opposed to achieving gains. According to the standard theory, utility depends only on the level of wealth, not how you got there. Loss aversion depends on a reference point. Two identical individuals who ended up with an investment worth $1,000 would differ in their perceived happiness if one started with $2,000 and the other started with $500. Loss aversion causes investors to hold losers to avoid the experience of taking a loss and to realize gains. This is precisely the opposite of what the tax timing option says that a rational investor should do.

Overconfidence

Overconfidence was one of the first biases suggested by behavioral financial economists. One example of overconfidence bias is that people do a poor job of estimating probabilities but still believe that they do it well. As a result, they fail to properly assess investment risk. Another example is failure to recognize that every trade involves a counterparty and that that counterparty may be more informed than you. Finally, overconfidence can lead to a failure to diversify because the investor falsely believes that he or she can identify mispriced securities.

Self-Control Bias

Self-control bias is a bias in which people fail to properly pursue long-terms goals because of a lack of self-discipline. The prime example behaviorists offer is the failure to allocate wealth properly over time, particularly in failing to save adequately for retirement.

Status-Quo Bias

Status-quo bias is a bias that causes people to do nothing rather than respond properly to changing circumstances. An example is failing to react to the impact of security price changes over time. What was originally a well-diversified portfolio may become much less so if a few securities rise very sharply over time. A person suffering from status-quo bias would continue to hold the original portfolio rather than reallocating to increase diversification.

Endowment Bias

Endowment bias arises when an investor values an asset more highly when they hold it than when they do not. People who suffer from endowment bias violate the rational principle that the price that a person is willing to pay for a good should equal the price at which they are willing to sell it. Endowment bias can lead people to fail to realize losses to take advantage of the tax timing option and to fail to reallocate their portfolio to properly manage risk.

BEHAVIORAL FINANCE AND MARKET PRICING

In Chapter 2, we introduced two key investment concepts: Bill Sharpe's arithmetic and the efficient market hypothesis. If we now add the possibility of irrational behavior, it is natural to ask how it affects both. To begin, behavioral finance has *no implications* for Bill Sharpe's arithmetic whatsoever. This may seem surprising until you remember that Sharpe's analysis was not based on any assumption about investor behavior; it was based exclusively on the tautology that all securities must be held. That conclusion clearly holds in any market, no matter how irrational the participants. In addition, the implications of Sharpe's analysis remain unchanged. No matter the degree of irrationality, it is still the case that passive investors as a group will outperform active investors as group and that individual active investors can outperform only at the expense of other active investors.

Behavioral finance is, however, an attack on the efficient market hypothesis. In fact, the genesis of the field was early research attempting to explain stock price anomalies that appeared to be inconsistent with market efficiency. One of the first preeminent papers in this regard was the work of DeBondt and Thaler. They found that when stocks are ranked on past returns, past winners tend to underperform and vice versa for past losers. DeBondt and Thaler attributed these reversals, which are inconsistent with market efficiency, to investor overreaction. They argued that in forming expectations, investors give too much weight to the past performance of firms. Such a tendency to place too much weight on recent past performance is consistent with several of the biases discussed above.

The first problem in assessing the reliability of results like those reported by DeBondt and Thaler is confirming that the anomalies really exist. Like the search for risk factors, the rise of behavioral finance set off a massive search for "anomalies." As we noted in Chapter 7, such searches are sure to find anomalies even in a random data set due to data mining. Remember that market efficiency does not mean market perfection. In some cases things will turn out better than the market expected and in other cases worse. This is not an anomaly – just the result of the unpredictable random variation in asset prices.

This point is made in a stinging response to the early research in behavioral finance by Eugene Fama. Prof. Fama, like Leo Tolstoy, notes that there is a veritable zoo of behavioral biases and associated anomalies. Some predict overreaction, some predict underreaction, and so forth. Fama finds that taken as a whole, the predicted anomalies are often contradictory. For instance, DeBondt and Thaler explain the winner–loser anomaly as resulting from overreaction. But there are other behavioral studies which find anomalies that are explained as resulting from underreaction. How do the behaviorists decide when investors overreact and when they underreact? And what is the net effect, if any, on market price from the interaction of all the errors and biases exhibited by all of the investors in the market? In Fama's opinion, the evidence shows that any net effect is weak at best.

Fama also finds that while behavioral models work well on the specific anomaly they were designed to explain, they fail to offer insight into other anomalies. This is what one would expect to see if the anomaly was an artifact of data mining. Similarly, Fama finds that the anomalies are highly sensitive to the model used to determine whether there was in fact an anomaly in the first place. This is the bad model problem also discussed in Chapter 7. Fama observes that if a reasonable change in the method of estimating superior returns causes an anomaly to disappear, the anomaly is on shaky footing and may well be an illusion. He offers evidence that such is indeed the case.

When you put it all together, it is unclear what behavioral finance has to say about mispricing other than to warn investors that markets may not be as efficient as the textbook theory suggests because individual investors are subject to behavioral errors and biases. The final obstacle to the hypothesis that errors and biases affect market prices is that modern financial markets are dominated by institutions, not individuals. Unless the institutions exhibit the same errors and biases as individual investors, or unless institutions face constraints that prevent them from arbitraging away biases caused by individual investors, there is little reason to believe that market prices would be meaningfully affected.

INDIVIDUALS VERSUS ORGANIZATIONS

All the departures from rational utility maximization that behaviorists point to, apply at the level of individuals. The experiments that led to the discovery of the irrational behavior, such as the classic work of Kahneman and Tversky, and Thaler, were typically done in a university setting with college students as subjects. For the discovered behavioral errors and biases to affect market prices, it must be due to the investment decisions of active individual investors. Passive individual investors do not have an impact because they passively hold the market portfolio. But as we have seen, active individual investors play a small and decreasing role in financial markets.

With regard to sophisticated institutional investors, there is no reason to believe they would exhibit the same errors and biases as individuals. To begin with, these organizations are designed to be as effective as possible in identifying and exploiting mispricing. Rather than relying on reactions of individuals, they put in place procedures that involve systematic analysis, cross checking, and group decision-making, among other things. It is also likely that the biases listed in the taxonomy would be self-canceling, at least to a degree, within an organization. For instance, partner one may be overconfident that Tesla is overvalued, while partner two is overconfident that is undervalued. Partner three may frame an investment decision one way, while partner four frames it another. At meetings designed to make investment decisions, these competing biases would be discussed and ameliorated, if not eliminated. Furthermore, organizations are becoming increasingly reliant on electronic trading algorithms. In many cases, those algorithms have been specifically designed to identify and exploit pricing errors that might arise because of biases attributable to active human traders.

Unfortunately, the experiments that lie at the core of behavioral finance cannot be performed on sophisticated institutional investors because their entire investment decision-making process is proprietary. (As it must be if they hope to use it as a continuing basis for earning superior returns.) Our bottom line is that given the importance of institutional investors in the market place, it is unlikely that individual behavioral biases, even if they exist, have a significant impact on market prices.

The important role played by institutional investors is not lost on behavioral financial economists. Recognizing that sophisticated institutions would tend to offset pricing errors, they rely on the concept of limits to arbitrage to explain how individual biases might still affect market prices. In a classic paper published in 1997, Andrei Shleifer and Robert Vishny showed that investment firms attempting to "arbitrage away" behavioral mispricing would face the risk the mispricing could increase in the short run. If it did, capital could be withdrawn from their firm at precisely the wrong time, threatening the collapse of the company. The fate of Long-Term Capital Management described earlier is an example. Because of this risk, Shleifer and Vishny argue that arbitrage capital could be limited, allowing the errors and biases of individual investors to affect market prices.

The applicability of the Shleifer–Vishny argument depends on the relative size of those active individual investors who are affected by behavioral biases compared to professional investment firms that would attempt to arbitrage away the mispricing. When the Shleifer–Vishny article was published in 1997, Professor French reported that individual investors held 29.5% of U.S. stocks. By 2007, the last year for which Prof. French reported data in his Presidential Address, the fraction was down to 21.5%. In the decade since the publication of Prof. French's work, the fraction of stock held by individuals has dropped further, with the rise of exchange traded funds and hedge funds. And those individual stock holders include family offices run by professional investors, which are less likely to be subject to behavioral biases. In short, even if there are limits to arbitrage for investment firms, the size of professional holdings compared to the holdings of active individual investors has shifted to the point where it is hard to believe that limits to arbitrage would be sufficient to allow the behavioral foibles of individual investors to have a meaningful impact on market prices.

DOES IT MATTER WHY SECURITIES ARE . MISPRICED?

Behavioral finance is a theory designed to explain why the efficient market hypothesis would fail and discrepancies between market prices and fundamental values would arise. From the foregoing, you can see that we are skeptical of the view that individual errors and biases are likely to have a significant and persistent impact on market prices. But suppose we are wrong and the errors and biases do lead to meaningful mispricing. Does that have any practical implications for rational investors other than those we have already discussed? Our answer is no. The crucial question for such investors is not why a security is mispriced, but *whether* it is mispriced. In the chapter on fundamental analysis we already discussed how to answer that question. It requires estimating the fundamental value of a security and comparing it with the market price. That analysis does not depend on whether the mispricing is due to overconfidence, confirmation bias, or anything else. In fact, the effort to attempt to uncover the source of mispricing would be a time-consuming and expensive distraction for an investor who already must bear the costs of undertaking the fundamental valuation analysis.

The only way in which the source of the mispricing might enter the picture is in trying to assess how quickly the mispricing will be eliminated. If the mispricing is due to the market's failure to appreciate details regarding the performance of the business, then presumably the mispricing will be eliminated when financial results are reported. If the mispricing is due to behavioral bias, then presumably it could persist until that bias atrophies. Because the bias is by definition irrational, it is difficult to predict how long that could take. However, as new fundamental data about the business arrive, and as the valuation implications of that data become clear, the actions of rational investors, including institutions, will see that they are eventually reflected in market prices. For instance, the alleged "irrational exuberance" for tech stocks in the late 1990s eventually evaporated when the profits anticipated for most of the tech companies failed to materialize.

If we are right and behavioral errors and biases have little impact on market prices, does this mean they can be ignored? Not at all. Even in a perfectly efficient market, investors who suffer from behavior biases can make mistakes that impact their investment performance.

THE ROLE OF BEHAVIORAL BIASES IN AN EFFICIENT MARKET

To answer the question whether behavioral biases matter in an efficient market, it is necessary to ask, matter to whom? They would not matter to rational investors and sophisticated institutions. All that matters to such investors is whether or not prices are fair. But individual biases could matter a good deal to the people who exhibit the them. The problem would not be that the biased individuals could be exploited by selling them stocks at unfair prices. There are no stocks trading at unfair prices. But even when stocks are trading at fair prices, biased individuals can make important errors that will affect their investment performance. Below we list five of the most prominent.

Overtrading and Performance Chasing

Biases such as overconfidence, lack of self-control, and representativeness can all lead to excessive trading. In an efficient market, such trading only detracts from performance. The more active the trading, the greater the downward impact on the value of a portfolio. Fortunately for investors who exhibit this behavior, trading costs are low for individual stocks. A greater threat is chasing the performance of the successful active management strategy *du jour*. Investors who do this are likely to end up paying the maximum amount possible in fees and face added charges for moving into and out of funds.

Lack of Diversification

The same biases that lead to overtrading can also cause an investor to invest too much in a limited number of securities. Throughout this book, we have stressed the risk-reducing benefits of diversification. Investors who plunge into relatively few securities will bear risks for which the market does not offer a risk premium. In light of Prof. Bessembinder's work, such investors are likely to find themselves missing out on those securities that account for most of the value creation.

Excessive Market Timing

Although Shiller's cyclically adjusted P/E (CAPE) ratio appears to provide some indication of whether the market is "high" or "low," it is not a sufficiently accurate predictor to justify jumping in and out of the market on a regular basis. Most other known indicators fare no better. Therefore, if behavioral biases induce investors to move in and out of the market frequently, they bear the costs of moving in and out and their expected return is less when they are out of the market.

Failure to Properly Manage Taxes

Behavioral biases such as loss aversion can interfere with the ability to properly manage taxes. Recall that exploiting the tax timing option requires realizing losses and letting profits run. Loss aversion leads to the exact opposite behavior. The result is an unnecessarily high tax bill.

Failure to Allocate Wealth Properly Over Time

One problem the behaviorists have actively addressed is that many investors save too little for retirement. Behavioral economists Shlomo Benartzi and Richard Thaler have developed an entire program to address this problem. Their book *Nudge* is designed to help people cope with the biases that lead them to save too little.

This list is not exhaustive, but it makes the point. Even if markets are perfectly efficient, individual investors can make a host of mistakes that will hurt their performance. In this regard, individuals have a lot to learn from behavioral finance, even if it does not provide a tool for beating the market.

CONCEPTUAL FOUNDATION 8

Conceptual foundation 8 is that although behavioral economists have demonstrated that many people do not behave as rational utility maximizers in the fashion that the standard financial economic model assumes, it is less clear what, if any, implications this has for investing. In financial markets increasingly dominated by institutional investors, and with algorithmic trading technology playing a larger role, it is unlikely that arbitrage will fail to eliminate pricing errors caused by individual irrationality. Furthermore, what is important for investment decision-making is whether a security is mispriced, not why it is mispriced. That determination can be made without reference to behavioral finance. Finally, even if behavioral errors and biases do not affect market prices, investors who fall victim to them can make damaging investment mistakes such as overtrading and failing to diversify.

9

ALTERNATIVE INVESTMENTS

Thus far we focused on publicly traded stocks and bonds of developed countries, primarily the United States. Although these are the most important assets for investors to consider, the number of alternative investment candidates runs into thousands. To begin, there are the major categories of alternate investments. These include the stocks and bonds of developing countries, real estate, commodities, and investments in private companies. Next there are an untold number of derivatives securities. Finally, there are more exotic investments including precious metals, jewelry, art, collectibles, and the current star of the exotic investment show – cryptocurrencies. With such a large menu of alternative assets, in any given year a few are going to do extremely well.[1]

---

[1] Of course, some will do extremely poorly as well, but those tend to get less publicity.

The astonishing increase in the price of Bitcoin in 2017 is an example.

Aside from direct investment in alternatives, there is now a large menu of funds that hold alternative investments and offer shares or partnership interests to the public. For instance, there are exchange traded funds (ETFs) that track oil, gas, gold, and silver.

The plethora of alternatives is likely to leave most investors feeling frustrated because there will always be a fantastic performer they missed. For instance, at SMBP we have avoided investing in Bitcoin because in our view it has little fundamental value. Nonetheless, we still find ourselves saying, "What if we had bought Bitcoin when it was less than $100?" That type of thinking is a grave danger. It encourages investors to chase the star investment of the day rather than designing and holding a well-balanced portfolio. The financial media add to the danger by an almost obsessive focus on the hot asset *du jour*.

Our basic message on alternative investments is to ignore the noise and accept the fact that you are always likely to feel bad about missing this year's hot investment. The good news is you will also miss the hot investment idea of last year that collapsed this year.

An important question to ask when considering alternative investments is: What is gained by adding alternative investments to a diversified portfolio of stocks and bonds? A bad answer is: Higher expected return. There is no evidence that any of the alternative asset classes offer better risk-adjusted returns than stocks and bonds. It may not appear that this is the case because, as noted above, there always seems to be some hot asset class, currently cryptocurrencies, that has experienced an extraordinary run-up. But just as monkeys at typewriters will eventually produce a novel, if you have enough alternative investments, one will always make stock and bond returns look meager. But the next year, it will be another one. A better answer is that adding alternative investments increases diversification and, thereby, reduces risk. However, if an investor is already holding a highly diversified portfolio of stocks and bonds, the added diversification benefits are limited. In short, we do not think alternative investments should constitute more than a sliver of the typical investor's portfolio.

Despite our general advice to ignore most alternative assets, it may be reasonable to invest small amounts in the primary categories of alternative assets: real estate assets, developing country stock, private equity shares, and commodities. For all but very large investors, the only reasonable way to hold these alternative investments is through funds. The reasons are related to four issues: liquidity, information, property rights, and necessary management. To some extent they all interact. We consider each below.

LIQUIDITY

Liquidity is a tricky concept. Some people say that an asset is liquid if it can be sold quickly, but that definition does not work. Consider your home. Could you sell it quickly? Sure, if you asked a price 10% of its appraised value you could sell it instantly. By this first definition, every asset is liquid if the price is low enough.

A more sophisticated definition is that an asset is liquid if you could sell it quickly at the market price. If there is a quoted bid-ask spread, that is a good way to measure liquidity. The size of the spread represents the price that counterparties charge for making a market for you. In the case of actively traded common stocks, we saw that the charge was tiny – or the order of 0.05%. Unless you have a huge block of shares, you can sell them virtually instantaneously within a whisker of the market price. However, we also noted that as you move away from situations in which there is an active, transparent market, liquidity becomes more difficult to define. For instance, does it make sense to speak of the bid-ask spread on your house? Suppose, for example, that based on comparable sales your house is worth $500 000. If you wanted to sell it within a day, you would probably have to take a big haircut. In that sense, the bid-ask spread is large. But if you are willing to wait six months, the haircut could be minimal. This illustrates that in a less active market, the spread is likely to be a function of the time taken to market the asset.

Because being able to sell assets quickly without taking a haircut is valuable to investors, more liquid assets will sell at higher prices. One of the big issues in business appraisal is how to estimate the illiquidity, or lack of marketability, discount associated with private companies. It is not uncommon for business appraisers to apply marketability discounts of 25% or more depending on the facts and circumstances involved. Those discounts translate into higher expected returns for investors who are willing and able to hold illiquid assets. Warren Buffett's Berkshire Hathaway is a perfect example of how wealthy, patient investors can harvest the illiquidity premium. Because Berkshire has large cash reserves, Mr. Buffett can buy illiquid assets and hold them without the fear of having to liquidate them at an inopportune time. He can also ride out so-called liquidity crises. Crises arise because illiquid assets tend to become even more illiquid during bad times. At the height of the financial crisis, for instance, markets for mortgage-backed securities, which were previously quite liquid, virtually dried up. Organizations that had to sell the securities during the crisis were forced to accept fire-sale prices. Mr. Buffett does not have to worry about selling at the wrong time because Berkshire Hathaway is effectively an exchange traded fund. Holders of Berkshire stock who need money in bad times can sell the stock without Mr. Buffett having to sell the underlying assets.

Illiquid assets are also hard to value for reporting purposes. If an ETF holds the S&P 500 stocks, it knows the value of all of its holdings at the close of business each day. For instance, at the close of business on December 15, 2017, the Vanguard S&P 500 ETF reported a net asset value (NAV) of $383.4 billion dollars. If a fund holds shopping centers scattered around the nation, most of which have not traded in years, how does it report its NAV? The answer is that it relies largely on appraised values. But appraised values can diverge sharply from market prices, particularly in bad times. An example is Vornado Realty Trust, which owns 86 large properties primarily in the New York area. Because the Trust is listed on the New York Stock Exchange (NYSE), the shares are liquid and the market capitalization of the equity is known (it was $14.8 billion on December 15, 2017). However, the market value of the underlying properties is unknown.

Another problem with real estate related to its liquidity is that it is lumpy. You can't buy 10% of a commercial building (other than by forming a partnership.) This makes it impossible for all but very large investors to hold a reasonably diversified portfolio of real estate.

INFORMATION

For a major American company like Apple, it can be argued that there is too much information. Dozens of analysts follow the company. In addition, the Internet is filled with speculation and rumors about future products. The financial media speculates interminably about whether or not it is a good time to buy or sell the stock.

The same is not true of Qihoo 360, a Chinese software company started in Beijing in 2005. Whereas a buyer of Apple can be confident the stock price is fair due to a combination of widely available information and a highly competitive stock market, can a purchaser of Qihoo 360 share that confidence? Probably not. And if you could, how would you know? Furthermore, as a foreign buyer of a small Chinese company, how could you assure yourself that you are not the counterparty to an informed trader on the other side?

As with American stocks, many of these information problems can be eliminated by passively holding a widely diversified index. For instance, holding a passive index eliminates the counterparty risk. There remains, however, concern that the entire market may be subject to booms and busts based on political developments, which are difficult for foreign investors to anticipate.

The same is true to a degree with U.S. real estate assets. To monitor its investment in a Portland commercial building, employees of SMBP had to make periodic trips to talk to tenants, meet with City officials, and walk through the neighborhood. There was no Apple-like flow of free information; all this effort was costly. Our analysis revealed that after taking account of the information costs, as well as all the costs of operating the property, the returns SMBP could expect to earn were less than those on the S&P 500.

The bottom line is that for many alternative assets, proper management and investment decision-making involve bearing unavoidable information costs. Funds may be able to take advantage of economies of scale to reduce those costs on a pro rata basis, but they cannot be eliminated.

PROPERTY RIGHTS

Unless you have your own private army, owning something means relying on the legal system and the police to protect your property rights. When you own Apple stock, you count on the courts to enforce your rights to receive dividends and receive the proceeds from a sale. In the United States, these rights are taken for granted. In other parts of the world, particularly for foreign investors, property rights are less secure. Risks range from capital controls that prohibit taking funds out of the country to outright expropriation. For example, Venezuela expropriated oil project investments in the Orinoco Belt in 2007. These risks are virtually impossible for all but the largest individual investors to monitor and manage.

Related to property rights is the problem of corruption. Rather than insuring that investors receive the payments they are due, corrupt managers and politicians siphon off funds. The giant Brazilian oil company Petrobras paid out billions in bribes and kickbacks over the course of a decade. Parmalat, Italy's largest dairy company, went bankrupt in a $2.4 billion corruption scandal that nearly brought down the Italian government. Closer to home, Enron officials took huge salaries and bonuses on the basis of fake profits. Protecting property rights in many countries requires time and resources.

NECESSARY MANAGEMENT

At one point, SMBP had $5 million invested in Apple shares. At the time of the purchase, the Apple shares were added to SMBP's account and going forward the only thing to do was collect the dividends. No management was required. At another time, as noted earlier, we owned a $5 million commercial building in Portland, Oregon. The need for management was constant. There were problems with the tenants, maintenance difficulties, parking problems, regulatory issues, and so forth. We found that these ongoing management costs ate up much of the return on the investment.

One way to reduce the management costs is to take advantage of economies of scale by owning numerous properties. For instance, real estate investment trusts (REITs) reduce the pro rata costs of managing property by employing full-time staff with specialized skills to manage the properties. Despite such savings, however, managing real estate remains a costly undertaking.

What is true of real estate is also true of other alternative assets. Investing in stocks in Africa requires oversight and understanding of regulatory and political issues that do not arise in the case of U.S. equities.

Finally, private equity investments typically require the investor to become involved in the oversight and management of the companies in which it is a major investor.

In short, for many alternative assets there is no analog to the low-cost S&P 500 ETF, in which the only management required at the fund is record keeping and the trading of liquid assets to match the performance of the index.

MEASURING RISK AND RETURN

If alternative assets are encumbered with the foregoing impediments, then shouldn't there be compensation in the form of higher returns in a competitive market? The question is not an easy one to answer because issues like illiquidity make it hard to measure investment performance with precision. Remember that proper measurement of risk and return requires periodic observation of the market value of the asset. For instance, our analysis of stock risk and return used either daily or monthly returns. The fact that data are not available for many alternative assets makes the measurement of both risk and return less accurate. Nonetheless, the academic research that has been done indicates that assets that are less liquid, have less available information, and require more management do reward their holders with higher average returns. Whether they are higher on a risk-adjusted basis after considering all the information and management costs is an even more difficult question to answer because risk and return are so hard to measure for these assets. There does, however, appear to be evidence that even on a risk-adjusted basis, alternative assets offer superior returns, but only for the lowest-cost, most efficient investors like Berkshire Hathaway.

Turning to risk, the apparent benefits of added diversification are not as large as they appear at first blush. The reason is that American companies own real estate, do business internationally, and depend upon commodities as part of their business activity. Therefore, holding a passive market index of American stocks already includes effective investment in real estate, commodities, and international business. As a result, the impact of adding explicit alternative investments in these areas does not have a major impact on the degree of diversification of a market index-based portfolio.

In most cases, the performance of the underlying assets is not what matters to final investors because they will typically hold fund shares and not the underlying assets. That makes quite a difference, because unlike the underlying assets, fund shares are typically not illiquid and no management is required to hold them. If there are superior returns to be earned from owning the underlying assets, much of the benefit is likely to be captured at the level of the fund and reflected in fees, salaries, and operating expenses. Even if some of the excess returns are passed through to shareholders, the price of the fund shares will be bid up to reflect the higher expected returns on the underlying assets, so that the investors who buy the shares receive only a fair risk-adjusted rate of return. This is analogous to what happens with normal common stocks. For instance, Apple makes superior returns on its operating investments, but the price of the stock is bid up so that shareholders make only fair returns. This is the good news/bad news aspect of holding shares in a fund (or a company) rather than owning the underlying assets. Owning the shares overcomes the difficulties associated with owning the underlying assets, but at the cost of foregoing the higher expected returns.

With that background, we now take a quick look at some of the ways that investors can hold alternative assets through funds and point out some of the issues involved.

REITs

One of the largest and most important alternative assets is real estate. Because real estate is illiquid and lumpy, the only reasonable way for most investors to hold a diversified portfolio of real estate is through a fund. The most common funds by far are real estate investment trusts, or REITs. Effectively, REITs were ETFs before there were ETFs, but there are a few differences. Because REITs are required to distribute 90% of their taxable income to investors, they must rely upon external funding as their key source of capital. Publicly traded REITs raise funds via an initial public offering and use those funds to buy, develop, and manage real estate assets. As with other ETFs, shareholders own a portion of a managed pool of real estate. Income is generated through renting, leasing, or selling the properties and is distributed directly to the REIT holder on a regular basis. When a REIT pays out its dividends, they are equally distributed among shareholders as a percentage of paid-out taxable income.

Like ETFs, REITs are a great way to hold illiquid assets because the REIT does not have to sell the underlying real estate when investors need cash. Cash-hungry investors can sell their shares to other investors. However, this makes it difficult to determine the market value of the REIT's assets. Because the properties trade infrequently, market data is rarely available. REITs attempt to overcome this problem by having the properties appraised. But the cost of appraisals means they are done infrequently and in any event, appraisals are an imperfect substitute for market prices.

REITs also economize on management costs by taking advantage of the economies of scale associated with holding a large portfolio of properties. Because REITs are operated by real estate professionals, the information problem is also ameliorated. For investors who wish to diversify into real estate, REITs are a reasonable and relatively cost-effective way to do so.

DEVELOPING COUNTRY FUNDS

Originally virtually all developing country funds were actively managed in order to cope with the liquidity, information, and property rights issues discussed above. However, in the past two decades financial markets in developing countries have grown dramatically. This has led to the appearance of low-cost, passive funds that invest in developing country equity. A good example is the Vanguard FTSE Emerging Markets ETF.[2] The fund invests in stocks of companies located in emerging markets around the world. The goal of the fund is to closely track the return of the FTSE Emerging Markets All Cap China A Inclusion index. Currently, the fund holds shares of 4726 companies and has a market value of $16.3 billion. Vanguard is able to operate the fund with a remarkably low expense ratio of 0.14%, or 14 basis points. Funds like this make it easy and inexpensive for even small investors to gain exposure to developing country stock markets.

When investing in emerging market stocks, bear in mind that an optimally diversified stock portfolio should be weighted according

---

[2]FTSE is an acronym for the Financial Times Stock Exchange Index.

EXHIBIT 9.1 Make-up of the world stock market by country: 2003 and 2016.

Market	Market Cap (US$ trillion) October 2016	Market Cap (US$ trillion) October 2003	% Change	% of Total 2016	% of Total 2003
U.S.	23.80	12.70	87	36.3	45.2
China	6.60	0.42	1471	10.1	1.5
Japan	5.20	3.10	68	7.9	11.0
Hong Kong	4.10	0.83	394	6.3	3.0
U.K.	3.00	2.20	36	4.6	7.8
Canada	1.90	0.74	157	2.9	2.6
France	1.90	1.30	46	2.9	4.6
Germany	1.80	0.94	91	2.7	3.3
India	1.70	0.23	639	2.6	0.8
Switzerland	1.40	0.66	112	2.1	2.3
Top 10	51.40	23.12	122	78.4	82.3
World	65.60	28.10	133	100.0	100.0

to market values. Exhibit 9.1 provides data on the ranking of world stock markets. Note that while the U.S. market remains the world's largest by a large margin, the margin is shrinking, primarily because of the dramatic growth in the Chinese market. According to Bloomberg, in 2003 the United States accounted for 45.2% of the value of world stocks. By 2016, the U.S. fraction had reduced to 36.3% of the total, in large part because China had rocketed from 1.5% to 10.1%. Between 2003 and 2016, the aggregate value of Chinese stocks rose by 1,479%. Given the growth in the Chinese market, Vanguard may have to stop referring to China as an emerging market.

The exhibit also shows that the top ten markets accounted for about 80% of the total in both 2003 and 2016. This implies that the stocks of true emerging markets like Brazil and India should remain a small fraction of an investor's portfolio.

PRIVATE EQUITY FIRMS

Given the management time and expertise associated with owning part or all of private companies, the only reasonable way for investors to get exposure to this sector is through private equity firms. The problem with these firms, as we noted in Chapter 6, is that they are expensive (with one great exception that we discuss below). In addition, because they are typically organized as unregistered partnerships, so the number of investors is limited to 99 and the required size of investment is correspondingly large. As a result, few individuals are investors in private equity firms.

The exception is Berkshire Hathaway. Berkshire is not often thought of as a private equity firm, but from an economic standpoint that is what it has become – the world's largest and cheapest private equity firm. In the last 20 years, a majority of the investments made by Mr. Buffett and Mr. Munger have been entire companies, or big parts of companies, the largest being the $45 billion acquisition of Burlington Northern Railroad. Other major acquisitions in the last decade include Marmon Group, Lubrizol, and Clayton Homes.

The good news is that Berkshire is the least expensive private equity firm on the planet. Mr. Buffett and Mr. Munger draw salaries of only $100,000. Their vast wealth has come from appreciation of the shares they hold. The headquarters of Berkshire in Omaha employs only 25 staffers. Of course, the entire company employs about 360,000 people, but those are in-line jobs making money for shareholders. There are no special fees charged as "a percentage of assets under management." Because Berkshire is Securities and Exchange Commission (SEC) registered and publicly traded, any investor can join Berkshire by buying shares and participating pro rata with Mr. Munger and Mr. Buffett. For a small investor looking for exposure to private equity, it is hard to recommend anything else.

FUNDS THAT MATCH COMMODITY AND OTHER INDEXES

With the dramatic expansion of ETFs, there are now funds tied to most any index you can think of. There are gold funds, oil funds, funds tied to the volatility of stock market, and the list goes on and on.[3] But there is an important hitch here. Recall that we noted that the Vanguard S&P 500 ETF almost identically tracked the S&P 500 index. You might guess that all passive funds tied to an index would work that way, but that conclusion is incorrect. As an example consider USO. The investment objective of USO is for the daily percentage changes in per share NAV to match the daily percentage changes in the spot price of light, sweet crude oil delivered to Cushing, Oklahoma. This seems to imply that the path of wealth (POW) from investing in USO would match the price path of West Texas crude oil as quoted in Cushing. The problem is that crude oil is expensive to store, so USO trades futures and swap contracts in order to attempt to match the daily percentage change in the price of West Texas crude. As a result, there is a slight slippage, which cumulates over time. Over an interval of days or weeks the slippage is not important, but for long-term passive investors it can be highly significant. As an illustration, Exhibit 9.2 plots the price of West Texas crude against a path of wealth (POW derived from the returns on USO). Although the patterns of the two lines look

---

[3]By the end of 2016, Bloomberg reports that worldwide there were over 6,000 ETFs and ETPs (exchange trade products) with over 12,000 listings and asset total 3.5 trillion in U.S. dollars.

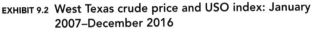

EXHIBIT 9.2 West Texas crude price and USO index: January 2007–December 2016

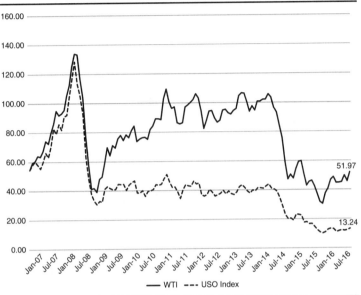

the same, the divergence between them slowly increases until by the end of 2016 the POW for USO is only about one-third of the West Texas crude price.

This behavior is not unique to oil ETFs. Many commodity funds and funds that attempt to replicate indexes have the same problem. It depends on whether the ETF actually holds the underlying commodity or has to rely on futures and swaps. If it holds the underlying commodity the ETF and the price index usually track closely. If a fund uses futures and swaps, tracking accuracy depends on how those contracts are priced. Without detailed knowledge of the relation between the futures and swaps and the underlying asset, investors should not assume that a long-term investment in an ETF will match the index. This makes them a poor choice for long-term investors.

DERIVATIVES

Derivatives have penetrated every nook and cranny of world financial markets. There are literally thousands of derivative products. The problem is that most of these derivatives involve implicit leverage and are complex and difficult to analyze. The "information" and skill necessary to properly evaluate them requires years to acquire. This makes them inappropriate investments for most all but the most sophisticated investors.

There is the alternative of holding derivatives through a specialized mutual fund or a hedge fund, but as we noted in Chapter 6, that is expensive. Furthermore, if the investor does not understand the underlying securities, how is he or she supposed to evaluate the fund that is holding them? The only option is to rely on track records, but as we have said repeatedly, track records are not a reliable indicator of future performance. For now, derivative securities are a poor choice for most investors.

THE EXOTICS

Cryptocurrencies are currently the poster child of this asset category, but it also includes gold, art, jewelry, collectibles, and other exotic assets. Our viewpoint on these exotics as investments can be summarized in two words: *avoid them*.[4] To one extent or another, they suffer from all of the problems we outlined at the start of this chapter. Unlike productive assets, they offer nothing in the way of pecuniary payouts. The best that can be said about them is that they may serve as a store of value in times of immense social upheaval.

---

[4]We say as investments because people may want to own art or jewelry for the enjoyment it provides. Perhaps calling it an investment makes it easier to spend the money.

Take, for instance, the case of cryptocurrencies. Their fundamental value can come from three sources: pecuniary payments to their holders (like interest on bonds), non-pecuniary convenience services (which for a currency is the ability to be used as a medium of exchange), and as a store of value. There is no dispute that cryptocurrencies do not offer a pecuniary return. They do not now, nor are there any plans for them to pay interest. With regard to their use as a medium of exchange they are dominated by traditional currencies. In addition, the costs of operating the blockchain make it unlikely they will replace traditional currencies as a medium of exchange any time soon. Finally, as a store of value they do have the property that the blockchain makes theft or expropriation very difficult. Laid against that, however, is the high price volatility which makes them an uncertain store of value. Taken as a whole, the inescapable conclusion is that cryptocurrencies have little fundamental value. Furthermore, whatever fundamental value they have now, they also had before the price ran-up by a factor of more than 100. This implies that the only explanation for the prices being paid today is that people believe the price will be higher tomorrow. Because we believe that investments should be justified by the fundamental value of the assets being purchased, it is clear why our recommendation is to avoid cryptocurrencies.

CONCEPTUAL FOUNDATION 9

Although there are thousands of alternative assets, in addition to the stocks and bonds issued by companies in developed countries, the benefits to investors of holding them are limited. With the exception of real estate and the stocks of developing countries, our view is that all but the most sophisticated investors should avoid alternative assets. There is scant evidence that holding them increases risk-adjusted expected returns and the benefits associated with added diversification are limited.

Because there are so many types of alternative assets, in any given year one type or another will be an exceptional performer. In 2017, it was cryptocurrencies. Chasing the star performer *du jour* is likely to distract an investor from the more appropriate long-term approach of buying and holding a well-diversified portfolio.

10

INVESTMENT SUGGESTIONS AND POSTSCRIPT

We would be remiss to write an entire book on investing and end it without offering investment suggestions. One problem with so doing is that everyone is different. They have different skills, disparate knowledge, differing net worth, different risk aversion, and different tax liabilities. All those factors will affect the optimal choice of investments. Therefore, the best we can do is offer some broad advice and leave it to the reader to fill in the gaps.

Perhaps the most important advice we can offer is, "Know thyself." Or even better, in the words of Clint Eastwood's Dirty Harry in the movie *Magnum Force*, "Man's got to know his limitations." The most dangerous thing in investing is thinking you know things that you don't know. Bill Sharpe's arithmetic drives that point home. If you think you are a superior active investor, then you are concluding that you can make those superior profits at the expense of counterparties who are also active investors. Is that a reasonable conclusion? If you cannot answer yes, then the best path is a probably a passive investment strategy. In that context, our first suggestion is to follow what we call a diversified passive strategy.

A DIVERSIFIED PASSIVE STRATEGY

In his letter to shareholders, Warren Buffett recommended that most investors are well advised to passively hold the S&P 500. We basically agree with Mr. Buffett, but think that a more diversified passive strategy would be a better solution for most investors for several reasons. First, there is no need to limit the passive holdings of U.S. stocks to the S&P 500. Low-cost exchange traded funds (ETFs) make it easy to add smaller U.S. companies to an investor's portfolio. For instance, Vanguard offers a total U.S. stock market ETF that is based on the entire Center for Research in Securities Prices (CRSP) index as well as an S&P 500 ETF. In point of fact, the two funds behave very similarly because the 500 stocks in the S&P 500 constitute most of the value of the CRSP index, but there is still some benefit to the greater diversification.

There is also benefit to international diversification. Once again low-cost ETFs and other passive funds make this relatively inexpensive. Good options include funds that invest in Europe, Asia, and developing markets. At SMBP, we currently limit the international exposure to 20% of the value of the portfolio, but are considering an increase as the world stock market grows relative to the U.S. market.

Depending on taxes and risk preferences, investors will also want to consider fixed income funds. Vanguard has a menu of several dozen to choose from including Treasury, corporate, tax-exempt, and low-grade bond funds. A commonly recommended portfolio is 60% equity, 40% fixed income, but there is nothing magic about that. Each investor should make his or her own decision.

Finally, real estate investment trusts (REITs), ETFs, and other specialized funds make it feasible for even small individual investors to hold alternative assets. Real estate, stocks of developing countries, and commodities are the most likely candidates here. Some would argue that cryptocurrencies deserve a place at the table here as well, but from our perspective their current high price and lack of any clear fundamental value make them a poor choice at the present time. In addition, for the reasons discussed in Chapter 9, we suggest caution when investing in any of these alternative assets, even via funds. First, the illiquid nature of many alternative assets makes it hard to value a fund that holds them. Second, it is not clear that the funds can be truly passive because management is required to operate assets like real estate. Third, there are potential information costs. Finally, funds do not always match the long-term performance of the index they are tracking. For all of these reasons, we would limit investment in such alternative assets to less than 10% of an overall portfolio.

The benefits of such a diversified passive strategy are worth reviewing. The first, as we just emphasized, is diversification. Via diversification, the investor avoids bearing risks that are not compensated with added expected return. The second is low costs and fees. As we have stressed, investment performance goes up and down but costs and fees are constant. Even costs and fees of 1% per year have a significant impact on long-term wealth accumulation. The third is that the passive strategy eliminates the temptation to overtrade based on false perceptions of mispricing. Such overtrading could take the form of buying and selling individual stocks or trying to time the market. Finally, a diversified passive strategy prevents an investor from becoming the counterparty to other active investors with better information and analytical skills. All in all, it is hard to argue with the viewpoint that a diversified passive strategy is the best choice for most investors.

AN ACTIVE STRATEGY

For investors who want to pursue an active strategy, our advice is that it must be based on detailed fundamental analysis. The goal should be to discover and hold for protracted periods those investments that the investor's analysis suggests are mispriced. This is effectively the strategy that Warren Buffett pursues. The problem is that while the strategy is easy to state in principle, it is devilishly difficult to implement in practice. It requires an ability to value companies more accurately than the market and that is no simple task. Like any specialized skill, becoming a talented fundamental investor requires years of training and experience. It also requires the confidence and the patience to stay with a position through the market gyrations that are sure to occur and to recognize that if the market is irrational today it could become more irrational tomorrow.

If you have read this book and concluded that we are reluctant to recommend an active strategy, you are right. We agree with Mr. Buffett that active strategies are not good choices for most investors and fear that there is far too much suggestive commentary and even explicit marketing that attempt to convince investors that they are good choices. Most people would recognize immediately that they cannot suddenly become professional golfers. The same thinking should apply to active investing. We urge you to proceed with caution.

USING ACTIVE INVESTMENT MANAGERS

An alternative to actively managing your own money is to place funds with active managers. This provides the same diversification benefits as holding passive funds along with the possibility of beating the market. Nonetheless, we have significant concerns with this approach.

The first is that it substitutes choosing a manager for choosing securities. In many ways, it is more difficult to select a manager than to evaluate a security. A security can be evaluated via a fundamental valuation model, but a manager cannot. The manager typically holds hundreds of securities which are constantly turning over. Consequently, the only way to evaluate a manager is by understanding their investment philosophy and examining their track record. Understanding the investment philosophy puts the investor right back in the position of having to make complex assessments of the underlying investments. With regard to track records, as we have shown in previous chapters, track records of three years or less have virtually no predictive power regarding how a manager will perform in the future. To the extent that track records do have some predictive power, past winners tend to be future losers. How many investors would be comfortable selecting a manager with a bad track record? Finally, given the high short-term variation in performance across competing funds, there is a tendency for investors to constantly move money into the star fund of the day. Academic research suggests that such performance chasing adds to cost without any offsetting benefit.

The second issue is cost. Active management ranges from expensive to very expensive in the case of hedge funds and funds of funds. Unless the investor can identify funds that outperform the market sufficiently to cover the costs with a margin of superiority left over for the investor, active managers will perform worse than passive managers. This is the most common outcome.

Our conclusion is that for most investors passive investing trumps active investing. Once a portfolio has been designed there is no need for constant evaluation and second guessing. In addition, the benefits of the lower costs are certain to accumulate over time.

AN "ENHANCED" PASSIVE STRATEGY

If the temptation to manage your own money is too strong to overcome entirely, the best solution could be a mixed strategy combining both passive and active. That is the strategy we employ at SMBP. The core of the SMBP portfolio is a series of low-cost ETFs, but they are complemented by positions in individual securities and derivatives to take advantage of what we perceive to be mispricing. We also use derivatives to alter our exposure to the overall market, depending on our assessment of whether stock prices are "rich" or "cheap" according to a variety of indicators including Prof. Shiller's CAPE. As we write this, the passive portion of SMBP's portfolio is large because, in our view, stock prices are so high that there few attractive opportunities on the long side and we are unwilling to take too many positions (like Tesla) on the short side. We also have reduced our exposure to the level of the market, and hopefully added to the portfolio return, by writing options on stock indexes. However, the option writing has been limited because the extremely low volatility of stock prices means that option premiums are small.

Of course, the approach taken at SMBP is just one way to enhance a diversified passive strategy. The active portion of the portfolio will depend on the opinions of the investor. Every investor will have his or her own secret sauce.

We recommend that the investor track carefully how the active portion is affecting the return on the overall portfolio. One of the biases that behaviorists point to is giving oneself credit for outcomes that are largely determined by exogenous forces like overall movements in the market. Unfortunately, given the volatility of stock prices, assessing an investor's own active contribution is as difficult as assessing the performance of active managers. Nonetheless, tracking the impact of active decisions is a worthwhile undertaking if for no other reason than the fact that it helps get investors used to working with the tools of investment analysis including returns and paths of wealth. In our experience, most investors who do the analysis are surprised by the results.

CONCLUSION

To conclude, we often hear the phrase that "investing is as much an art as a science." As it stands, the phrase is little more than a platitude. What is worse, those words are often taken to mean there is little content to investment science. We hope that this book has helped convince you otherwise. Understanding the conceptual foundations of investing is a critical part of effectively managing your money. What is much less clear is the art part. After spending several decades in both the academic and practitioner worlds of finance, none of us has ever heard a coherent definition of "investment art." A more accurate statement would be that investing is an inexact science, but a science nonetheless.

POSTSCRIPT FEBRUARY 2018

Whenever you write a book there are two lags: one between the time you stop writing and the time the book is published and another between the time the book is published and the time the book is read. We completed writing this book just after the turn of the year in 2018. Unfortunately, markets wait for no one. To be as current as possible, therefore, we revisit a couple of the general suggestions we made in light of the most current information.

The most prominent example is bitcoin. In Chapter 5, we argued that the price of bitcoin of $15,749 in December of 2017 was difficult to explain as anything other than a bubble because bitcoin had no apparent fundamental value. If investors stopped believing that tomorrow's price was going to be higher than today's, there were no underlying cash flows that would support the price of bitcoin and sharp drops were likely to occur. It did not take long. By February 2018, the price of bitcoin had fallen below $6,000. This does not mean that the fever will never return, but we continue to believe an asset with no fundamental value is a poor investment at almost any price.

In Chapter 5, we also argued that the fact that the cyclically adjusted P/E (CAPE) ratio was a record high was a flashing red light suggesting that real stock returns over the next decade were likely to be below long-run historical averages. It did not take long for that weakness to emerge. Over the course of five trade days in February 2018, market indexes fell by more than 10%, constituting what is commonly referred to as a "correction." We don't want to make too much of this. As we stressed in Chapter 5, indicators like the CAPE ratio provide some information regarding average returns over the next decade. They have essentially no ability to predict sudden sharps drops in the market. Nonetheless, sharp drops are one way that decade-long returns fall short of expectations. While the February drop did lower the CAPE ratio, it still remains near record territory. Therefore, this indicator still predicts lower real returns over the next decade. Whether that will be in the form of further short-term pain is unknown.

In Chapter 7, we introduced the concept of non-stationarity. The point made there is that not only are asset prices random, but the random probability distributions that describe prices can change as well. It is as if after drawing balls from one jug for a period of time, nature suddenly switches to a new jug. This possibility was driven home by the behavior of the VIX index in February 2018. After several years during which the index was near record lows and hardly moved from day to day, it suddenly jumped 100% in one day and tripled in the course of week. The moves were so pronounced that some exchange traded funds that were designed to profit from a low and stable VIX index, and that had been rising for years, collapsed and went bankrupt in a period of days. Nature was indeed drawing from a new jug.

INDEX